The Life we B

Good books

a Man called Ove / *my grandmother Told me To say she's sorry*

STREET-FIGHTING
LOGIC

Larry Crabb Soul Talk connect

The Art of Arguing with Grandmothers and Coffeeshop Philosophers

Expriencing God Blackaby Youth Edition

Brian G. Daigle

mud
h o u s e

Distributed from Baton Rouge, Louisiana by Mud House Art and Literature. Mud House Art and Literature is a non-profit distributor of visual art, original literature, and literature in the public domain.

Page design by Brian G. Daigle
Cover design by Brian G. Daigle
Cover art: detail of 'Piano Head' by Morbiim of Morbiim Fine Arts, Paint; Kenner, Louisiana, United States

Scripture quotations, unless otherwise indicated, are taken from the Holy Bible, English Standard Version. ESV text edition: 2007, copyright 2008 by Crossway Bibles; a publishing ministry of Good News Publishers.

Mud House Art and Literature titles may be purchased in bulk for educational, business, fund-raising, or sales promotional use. For information, please email MudHouseArt@gmail.com

Printed in the United States of America

For Kevin, a man of balance and strategy.

Table of Contents

Introduction

"True logic is not that noisy thing that deals all in dispute and wrangling, to which former ages had debased and confined it; yet its disciples must acknowledge also, that they are taught to vindicate and defend the truth, as well as search it out. True logic doth not require a long detail of hard words to amuse mankind, and to puff up the mind with empty sounds, and a pride of false learning; yet some distinctions and terms of art are necessary to range every idea in its proper class, and to keep our thoughts from confusion." Isaac Watts [1]

"The human brain is a machine for coming to conclusions; if it cannot come to conclusions it is rusty...Man can be defined as an animal that makes dogmas. As he piles doctrine on doctrine and conclusion on conclusion in the formation of some tremendous scheme of philosophy and religion, he is, in the only legitimate sense of which the expression is capable, becoming more and more human." G.K. Chesterton [2]

"...logic was made for man, not man for logic." Peter Kreeft [3]

L ike any introduction, this is a brief word to the reader. Welcome! Unlike other introductions, I intend to prevent you from reading the rest of this book, convincing you that this might be a great waste of your time. Take a hike. Run! Find something that will make you happy, comfortable even. If you are anything like me, you love your life. And if it does not kill us, learning has a tendency to change our lives, to turn us into those people we never thought we would become, which always has the lingering scent of our parents. If any subjects have this tendency to change us, they are the subjects dealt with in this meager six-by-nine lump of processed tree and cheap ink.

Here I will speak of reasoning, the kind Presidents use to win elections and the kind which makes a Starbucks barista move to make you a new peppermint latte. I will speak of art, the kind of art which makes us glory at the evidence that humans are the pinnacle of creation (as seen in Rembrandt) and the kind of art which presents humans as the irresolute climax of evolution's skin-and-bones lottery (as seen in Pollock). I will speak of stories, those rascally, necessary fancies which tend to provide an instant bone-marrow transplant as the words tickle our ear hairs and beat the drums, only to become ideas, the consequential kind. I will speak of conversation, a lost art amidst mounds of technophiliacs and social media*ites*. I will speak of grandmothers, and why their chocolate cake is sufficient warrant to believe there is a God. And, of course, I will speak of logic.

These are the characters in the story that is this book, and as I said at the start, you do not want to hear what I have to say about them. You do not want to hear whether I think they are the villain or the hero, and what kind of character you prove to be. These topics are too big. Too important. Too necessary for a life which is *actually* happy, as opposed to the kind we buy our children at the McDonald's drive-thru. Sorry, this book does not come with a toy. But it does come with calories. And I have been told that paper has some kind of nutritional value, especially for logs set ablaze by your neighbor's son. So, that is what you should do with this book. Set it ablaze before it does the same to you.

And for all you bookworms who turn to endless amounts of pages to solve life's ultimate problems, sorry; this too will let you down, like all the suitors who have gone before it. If this book does its job, it will not so much as create more problems *for* you as it will open your eyes to see more problems *around* and *in* you, problems that already existed, that can be solved nonetheless; problems which modern man, including many in the Church, has decided to either foolishly embrace or apathetically ignore. Don't say I didn't warn you. Run from this text while you are still alive, or at least unscathed.

It looks like it is too late. If you are reading this, you have read too far. Like mosquitoes on a bayou porch, you looked into the blue light for too long. You are committed. I wonder if you will make that same electrifying sound. We will know by the third chapter. If the story of you in this book ends with a loud *Zap!*, followed by the smell of burning insect wings and smoldering blood from your dog, two cats, and Aunt Myrtle, the least I can do is give you a heads-up as to what will happen before that wonderful display of redneck innovation. You are welcome. And as you ease closer to the bright, warm light of the MosquitoMuncher2000, do not be startled by the remains of those who have gone before you. They are in a better place. Learning tends to draw us in and kill us. Truth bids us come and die. Now to more cerebral lows, an introduction in the likeness of the others.

By nature, logic is a heady subject. It makes us think. It often makes us think so much it becomes easy to forget why we even study it. "Leave it to the braniacs!" they say. "What exactly does this have to do with *anything*?" is a common enough question heard in most logic courses or common conversations about logic. My goal with this text is to answer that exact question. No, not by dissecting more standard categorical syllogisms and filling in more truth-tables, rather I hope to answer it by giving specific and tangible applications toward an everyday practice of logic, a kind of informal practice of logic. And since we do not hold class in a café, on a street corner, or at your dinner table, the transfer of academic material to life's common scenarios can be that much more difficult, while no less important.

Originally, this book started as a four or five week culminating text of a two year logic curriculum. It was intended to fall at the end of an intermediate logic course, offering the students an opportunity to see logic in a new light, one that will allow a smooth transition to a formal study in rhetoric, for it is classically held that one should study logic before rhetoric, and it should be universally accepted that one should apply biblical wisdom to both at all times. My hope was, and still is, that this text bridges the gap between the often ethereal, cloudy classroom which occurs in any kind of philosophical discussion and the everyday, go-watch-the-Justin-Bieber-movie culture in which our students are immersed. If you have never taken a formal course on logic, or have not at least read a few good texts on logic, I would encourage you to do so now, before you go further here, as that foundation is immensely important for all that is to be said here. Without doing so, your efforts here will bear fruit, a quite shriveled and scrawny fruit with slight bruising and a few worm holes, but fruit nonetheless.

As is par for this kind of project, the more this text was breathed into existence the more the winds and waves shifted it onto a course of its own. While it started as a text for my students, it has shifted into a text addressed more broadly. At times the reader may find me speaking directly to my students, harkening back to certain lessons from class. Other times, the reader will find me speaking to a general audience. My hope is that my speech here will not only be edifying to the *yous* in the audience (my current and former students), but also those who are entering this theater for the first time, perhaps picking up a text on logic for the first time and subsequently probably having little desire for its formal use in education.

So far, if you have taken an introductory or intermediate logic course, most of your formal interaction with logic has consisted of things like identifying the truth-value of propositions or memorizing informal fallacies. These are absolutely crucial in learning the art of argument. But since humans are more than proposition-calculating machines or symbolic logic robots, and given that most of the world around us will have no clue as to what kind of extraterrestrial jargon we are speaking if we start using philosophical terms, we as proponents of logic-speak must find a way to transfer our technical terms to everyday scenarios. This is true of any subject dealing with a language specific to itself. Therefore, I have divided this book into four sections.

First, *the need* is imminent. Why do we study logic? What are the different applications of formal and informal logic? Why is it necessary to learn street-fighting logic? I hope to answer these questions by offering a brief critique of our 21st century, American culture and an explanation as to how we as Christians should reasonably engage this culture in its current form. I will also give an overview of logic in general and why it is a necessary good within any academic curriculum.

Second, *the training* is not a five-day diet or ninety-day fitness routine. Other than having some good, formal courses of logic under our belts, what are some other ways to prepare for employing street-fighting logic? Other than head knowledge of formal and informal logic, what other ways should Christians prepare to use logic in everyday encounters? The right use of logic consists of much more than passing a few classes. And if anything, passing a few logic classes should not be the culmination of our work in logic, but the beginning. The necessary training required for any logic student to excel is simple, but it is work. It is the kind of everyday work that could be compared to athletic training or vocational training. It is likewise surprisingly leisurely. In both its work and its leisure, the branch of philosophy we call logic is deeply rewarding. And it yields the kinds of rewards which permeate all areas of our lives – the spiritual, physical, emotional, *et cetera*. This training will not just change one's grade point average; it is meant to alter your relationship with your parents, your siblings, your teachers, and the random stranger sitting next to you at the Italian restaurant. It is meant to mature within you a certain kind of receptivity to the world and its inhabitants. It is the kind of training that is as much about relationship shaping as it is about worldview shaping.

The third section of this book, *the strategy*, is meant to give us gusto. Once an adequate amount of training has occurred, how should we go about practicing street-fighting logic? Which strategies are appropriate and which strategies are counterproductive? It does not matter how good a choir is at the fundamentals of music if they cannot perform the piece well. Strategy is the kind of thing that allows underdogs to take down behemoths. It is plan. It is execution. It is moment-by-moment decision making in the heat of the battle. It is poetic more than it is mechanical. It emerges more from *who we are* than from *what we know*. Strategy requires intuition. Without strategy, street-fighting logic becomes a guessing game; a kind of blind-man-playing-billiards scenario.

The fourth and final section, *the goal*, seeks to answer several important questions: why engage in street-fighting logic? With whom should I engage? When should I engage? What is the goal of my engagement? These questions must be supported by a kind of wisdom that often only comes with age and lots of on-the-job learning. Still, especially for the younger readers but certainly for all readers, we would do well to begin considering the answers to these questions. They are questions we should habitually ask ourselves, and questions we will learn how to more appropriately answer as we mature in interacting with people and picking up on interpersonal and social cues, gaining insight from further study of Scripture and our surrounding culture.

Regarding inspiration for this work, the 18th century Puritan Isaac Watts is woven in at nearly every possible turn. The reader will realize Watts's words and wisdom show up time and again. Though he may be known as the father of modern hymnody, Dr. Watts was one of the most copious, post-Reformation theologians. As a logician, Watts's *System of Logic* was used for many years as the primary text at both Oxford and Cambridge. He was a poet, philosopher, educator, catechist, and preacher. His critiques of John Locke's epistemology are as applicable in combating today's postmodern ideology as they were then in combatting

Enlightenment thinking. In preparing this book, he was of great help. I hope to use this present platform to pass his wisdom on to as many as will take it. Other great thinkers and those who spent their life well, contributing time and again to our present understanding of logic, are scattered throughout. Their work and influence upon, and recovery within, their posterity cannot be overstated.

In regards to those who deserve a special thanks, I appreciate Rod Olps's friendship and for first introducing me to the work and worth of Isaac Watts, without whom this present project would be but skin and bones. Thank you to Mr. Chuck and Mrs. Lisa Jarreau. Your home is a refuge, and you are a consistent model of Christian hospitality in allowing me to spread my study habits over your dining room table in writing and finishing this text. I also want to thank my Rhetoric students at Sequitur—Ruth Brown, Evan Chesney, Peyton Hendrix, Tysor Hanson, Hays Ward, Emily Winter, Thomas Wolff, and especially Nathanael Kazmierczak—for reading the manuscript and offering great insight to the project as a whole and its execution. Lastly, thank you to my wife, Lauren, whose countless pots of coffee have gone cold, because in the process of finishing this book I couldn't seem to walk away from the keyboard. And yet, like a faithful bride, you continued to brew one each afternoon.

Finally, and this is the part where your mosquito life begins to pass before your eyes: it is hard to separate logic from rhetoric. It is likewise quite difficult, nay impossible and pitiful, to separate logic from love. The content of an argument, the presentation of an argument, and the persons presenting and receiving the argument are not easily disentangled, if disentangled at all. So, this text will interweave these three great subjects – content, presentation, persons—as they are employed in everyday life. This text likewise seeks to act as a point of transition between formal logic and classical rhetoric. Simultaneously, I hope it serves those who have not taken a course in either. At its base, this book is littered with what will seem to be common sense, and usually it is. Yet, often times, common sense is not as common as we might expect. It helps to say common sensical things out loud, or as in this case, turn them into something you can throw into a winter's fire.

Furthermore, application is imperative. One can read, study, and listen to good things all hours of the day, but if we do not apply the lessons learned and allow ourselves to be formed by the information, then the subject has not really fulfilled its purpose. There is no subject for pure contemplation. Many of the philosophers lied to us. As my friend and colleague Kevin Lindholm is fond of saying, "If you want to appreciate music or art or literature, do not take an art appreciation class or a class on literature appreciation. Start making art. Read a good book! Learn an instrument!" We are embodied, social creatures. And we are created in the image of the Creator, which means we are to be creating *ex materia*. Therefore, all things we study should have an outward reality; one which makes solid objects around us move, homes smell like pumpkin spice, and animals even more dominated (in the Genesis 1 sense) to the point where we might even start a ridiculous clothing line for poodles. All subjects, especially those of an academic nature, imply a real-life application; logic arguably more so than others. So, this is intended to be a rubber-hitting-the-road, or a road-hitting-the-rubber, kind of book, depending on whether you are the rubber or the road, and whether you are a pacifist or an aggressor.

Logic should change our lives. It should change our love. It should change how we obey Jesus's great commission from Matthew 28: "All authority in heaven and on earth has been given to me. Go therefore and make disciples of all nations, baptizing them in the name of the Father and of the Son and of the Holy Spirit, teaching them to observe all that I have commanded you. And behold, I am with you always, to the end of the age." It should change how we treat our classmates, defend our faith, watch movies, listen to our favorite musician, listen to our least favorite musician, obey our parents, play sports, and even create new sports. As Christians we are commanded to "...love the Lord your God with all your heart and with all your soul and with all your mind and with all your strength...[and]...love your neighbor as yourself." (Mark 12:30-31) This is the chief end of all of life, of all that is in life. This is the chief end of street-fighting logic. So, sit. Relax. Stay a while, since you are already here. May your head be filled with the right kind of air and your fingertips know when to be the release valve. Just keep staring at the blue light. Your wings will do the fluttering. It isn't as harmful as you think. Death has a strange way of creating life; for the Christian, after death comes resurrection.

Brian Daigle
Baton Rouge, Winter 2014

Chapter 1
The Need

"Our society has replaced heroes with celebrities, the quest for a well-informed character with the search for a flat stomach, substance and depth with image and personality. In the political process, the makeup man is more important than the speech writer, and we approach the voting booth, not on the basis of a well-developed philosophy of what the state should be, but with a heart full of images, emotions, and slogans all packed into thirty-second sound bites." J.P. Moreland[4]

"The right to search for truth implies also a duty; one must not conceal any part of what one has recognized to be true." Albert Einstein Memorial in Washington D.C.[5]

"Once upon a time in Middle-Earth, two things were different: (1) most students learned 'the old logic,' and (2) they could think, read, write, organize, and argue much better than they can today. If you believe these two things are not connected, you probably believe storks bring babies." Peter Kreeft[6]

"The disrepute into which Formal Logic has fallen is entirely unjustified; and its neglect is the root cause of nearly all those disquieting symptoms which we may note in the modern intellectual constitution...to neglect the proper training of the reason is the best possible way to make it true, and to ensure the supremacy of the intuitive, irrational and unconscious elements in our make-up." Dorothy Sayers[7]

Historically, logic has been seen in countless colors. Some have seen it as a hindrance to higher realms. As Nicholas of Cusa once stated, "For a superabundance of Logic is injurious, rather than beneficial, to very sacred theology."[8] Others have seen it as a ladder to those same realms. Justin Martyr began his *First Apology* to the Emperor with an appeal to reason: "Reason directs those who are truly pious and philosophical to honour and love only what is true, declining to follow traditional opinions, if these be worthless. For not only does sound reason direct us to refuse the guidance of those who did or taught anything wrong, but it is incumbent on the lover of truth, by all means, and if death be threatened, even before his own life, to choose to do and say what is right."[9] Wherever we may stand on the issue, man's reasoning faculty has a unique and irreplaceable existence within each one of us, and especially in the history of Western thought.

Usually, and quite ironically, people do not want to hear a defense for why logic is important, either because they have no clue what logic is – and thus have no interest in its application to their particular world—or because they have already read a hundred other defenses. So, as I give my brief defense for why studying logic is a necessary good for all of us, I hope to either break the paradigms of the naysayers, which is more needed than they think, or be excessively repetitive for the yaysayers, which the apostle Paul sees, when rejoicing in good things, is itself a good thing, not grievous for me and a safeguard for you. (Phil. 3:1)

Some educators and parents I talk with need no *apologia* for why one should learn to use, and thus be trained in, good logic; either because they have already encountered a book which defends it, or, though they have not themselves read those books, they are already convinced of the arguments set forth in them. Others could use some fortification in knowing why we should have our children and our children's children take formal courses in logic, and consequently why the book you hold in your hand has any value whatsoever. Whichever you are, it would be helpful to know that logic has a tendency to defend itself, though it helps when we come alongside to explicitly point to its necessary presence within a healthy education and healthy society, and thus the formation of the good life. Logic has a kind of self-evident nature, one that is intuitively accessible and universally relevant. It is similar to studying physics. The laws of physics seem to be inherently beneficial, which we experience when we play sports, cook dinner, or read a book on gravity. Likewise, logic's goodness has been found, tasted, and continues to be the gift that keeps on giving. This chapter is for those who have not yet realized its goodness, or those who would like to taste it cooked and prepared a slightly different way.

The Forbidden Fruit of Being Human

As you may have already heard it said, the two things one should never talk about with family are politics and religion. Why? "Well," as the argument tends to go, "politics and religion are the two subjects that divide, and we don't want to be divisive among the people we are to love the most, do we?" Or, as another argument may postulate, "We argue year after year, just as soon as everyone has filled their red Solo cups with eggnog and their flimsy Dixie plates with heaps of Christmas finger foods, and we never come to any conclusions on the matter! It is just not worth it. Can't we all just get along?" Then, the conclusion follows: stay away from those topics. Keep it shallow, on the surface. You know, talk about sports, or the weather, or your grades, or how you broke your foot last month. Talk about anything. Just don't let the conversation tend toward those hideous dogmas of politics and religion. Then a holiday football bowl game is turned on and everybody drools with admiration.

While I have no problem discussing the simple things in life, the things Chesterton called tremendous trifles, and discussing them until we actually learn to give thanks for them, our culture has a tendency to never go beyond the surface. In this way, we can truly be called a superficial people. As J.P. Moreland goes on to say from the quote at the beginning of this chapter, "Three of the major centers of influence in our culture – the university, the media, and the government – are largely devoid of serious religious discussion."[10] The reason for this propensity, and consequently avoiding or marginalizing some of the nitty-gritty goodness of living in society, is two-fold: first, our culture really has bought into what Nancy Pearcey and others have identified as the 'fact-value split', where certain truths are publically accessible and others are mere private opinions. Certain topics, especially religion, have been labeled 'private opinion' or 'value'. These have been tossed out of the public square, where 'facts' alone have argumentative clout. More on this later. The second reason our culture lives on the surface, avoiding some of the more important concepts and discussions, is we have tended to form a false notion that to be tolerant of others' opinions and beliefs means neither challenging the validity of those beliefs nor ever having the pompous audacity to say they could *actually* be false. And of course, so the argument continues, how dare I ever make an institution based on principles which could judge or exclude others from communing in full, on their own terms. Well, contrary to how some may interpret the U.S. Constitution or the nature of religious beliefs, to call my neighbor's truth-claims false and dangerous for the continued health of a society is neither intolerant nor anti-freedom. Likewise, for someone to call *my* truth-claims false or dangerous to society is neither intolerant nor anti-freedom. To think so is to have a deep misconception of the nature of freedom, social tolerance, democracy, and religious beliefs. It is to be confused and self-refuting on a number of levels.

Functionally excluding discussions of religion or politics from public and private spheres has nothing whatsoever to do with either politics or religion being inherently divisive or wrong. In fact, it is politics and religion which tend to be the most unifying and restorative of human endeavors. The ancients were the first to recognize this and begin systematic tomes about it, Aristotle, Cicero, and Augustine in particular. There is nothing wrong with politics or religion as topics in themselves. Such thinking and living is wrong-headed, and is symptomatic of a larger illness. There is, however, something wrong with man, something wrong with how our modern culture tends to handle these topics and many others, no matter how small, including sports, ant farms, and eco-friendly design. There is a problem with our ability to carry on benevolent and edifying conversations and arguments about a topic with even our closest friend without getting overly defensive and unnecessarily hostile. Plus, it is not hard to find those who argue in order to fulfill their odd infatuation with conflict and self-exaltation, a manifestation of their desire to be altogether rebellious. This happens especially when they have taken a one-hundred level course on the subject from the local university, or at least listened to the radio program by someone who has. This is then paired with a kind of hyper-skepticism, producing a man whose intentions to argue are never pure. In a culture filled with this kind of citizen, and largely shaped by thirty-second sound bites and interruptions every two minutes, *serious* and *prolonged* discussions on important topics are hard to come by.

Public discourse and the ability to argue well, if they are not already dead, are dying arts in our culture, arts that must be healthy and maturing if a society itself is to survive and mature. This is one reason why many students in classical Christian schools read this book or get placed in their current educational setting. Many parents, educators, and clergy have realized this void and want their children to be good citizens in the city of God and the city of man, where being a good citizen has everything to do with how one communicates with others inside and outside of their immediate society. Whether a student becomes a lawyer, a police officer, a museum curator, or a stay-at-home mom, students cannot escape the reality of rhetoric and the abundant use of everyday logic. Properly employed arguments will change homes. They will change churches. They will change friends. They will change generations of people. Thus, learning to speak well in both the wisdom of delivery and soundness of argument is immensely important for all of life.

Still, it is not just Washington D.C. or Hollywood which suffer from an inability to think well. J.P. Moreland cites David Hazard's observation: "In too many churches, a questioning mind can be a plague to its owner. The thinking woman or man seldom gets much support today – and more often than not meets with resistance and suspicion. This is true, not only for those inclined to dig more deeply for a more reasoned, better-founded faith, but for the Christian who is laboring out in the world to resolve debates and value-clashes in fields like social justice, medical research, education, law, and finance."[11] To be a little more relevant to our students' generation, how would you describe your youth group at church? Is it filled with hearty conversation, a love for singing and learning, and a desire to both dance with your foes and dispute your friends? Do the students hold regular book clubs where they read the best literature from their civilization? Do they read the Church fathers with one another? Do they have movie critiques? Do they read and write poetry? Do their peers respect their parents more than they respect their boyfriend, girlfriend, or Facebook friend? Do they have Bible studies where they are matured as young men or young women in the great spiritual disciplines of our faith? Or are the students surrounded by flashing lights, game rooms, and cheap snacks? Is it constant commotion and loud music? Do the male mentors around the students speak with a biblical masculinity or are they indistinguishable from the middle school jocks or the lead guitarist of the trending emo band?

I am afraid many young Christians today would answer those questions in such a way as to affirm the latter and deny the former: we hold our children to a low standard of educational and spiritual maturity; we often times put before them insubstantial models for educational and spiritual maturity. That is unfortunate for and strange to the maturity of the Christian church. This is not only unbiblical, unfounded in Scripture, it is antithetical to Scripture. We must no longer confuse child-like faith with a self-imposed ignorance or naivety, or self-perpetuating immaturity. We must also no longer confuse maturity with a devour-the-whole-world-and-see-what-tastes-bad way of living. A lazy mind and an irresponsible heart are no spiritual, or physical, medals of honor. We should heed

J.P. Moreland's warning: "...the church's extinction will not come by sword or pillory, but by the quiet death of irrelevance."[12] And this irrelevance will not be because the students were out of touch with the latest clothing fashion or musical trends. This irrelevance will not happen because our churches were not seeker-friendly enough. The church's irrelevance will come precisely because we have sought to be *too* relevant, too concerned with cultural authenticity. We have befriended the seeker too much. What we have won the convert with, we have won him to. And *what* we have decided to win him *with* looks an awful lot like him. The Church's irrelevance will therefore be a kind of camouflage Christianity, a Christianity which has lost its ability to discern the holy from the profane and cogently defend with thought, word, and deed why the holy is worth our love and our lives.

Another place to probe within the Christian community is Christian schools. In the next day or so, head to your local Christian schools, all of them, and ask them for a brief breakdown of how much money is spent on sports and how much money is spent on a formal logic curriculum – teachers, materials, *et al.* How about how much money is spent on student computers and how much is spent on training and compensating a logic teacher? How about how much money is spent on deciding the color of the uniforms and deciding who will teach logic, or the amount of time pursuing success on standardized tests rather than pursuing success in mastering formal and informal logic. *Logic, because of its comprehensiveness and academic centrality, is the most important academic subject a student can master,* and yet our schools, especially our Christian schools, would be hard-pressed to put forth principals and school board members who can adequately define logic, much less who know where to start to offer it as a formal class at their school.

Another way the church is intellectually irrelevant is not just by its 'sins of intellectual omission' (what it does not teach), but by its 'sins of intellectual commission' (what it does teach). I recently had a student share with me a conversation he had with several adults at his church. "Logic is sin," my student said as he relayed the punch line given by the adult leading the class. According to my student's retelling of the story, the several adults in the Sunday school class got onto a soap-box about how reason is not of God, how logic is not faith, consequently placing it in the category of sin. As it turns out, this soap-box was slipperier than they realized. It should have been kicked out from underneath them with one, simple question: Why? Why is logic a sin? The irony of asking *this* question is that it cannot be answered without logic. And if the group believes that sin ought to be avoided, then of course their only path to faithfulness is silence, which does not seem like a bad option for these folks.

While it is rare in the Church to hear one speak with such hostility against logic, it is not rare to see logic treated as either the pinnacle of an unreachable mountain, only approachable by the elite few, or altogether unnecessary for faith, or even contra-faith. Popular sentiment in the West has never before placed 'faith' and 'rationality' at such great a distance from one another. This ought not be the case. We need a renewed understanding of logic, though ultimately we need a renewed understanding of the *Logos*, a clear vision of Jesus Christ, whom we may call God's apologetic and reason, God's premise and conclusion.

Defining Terms

As our students learn in the first few weeks of Introductory Logic, defining terms is important. So, let's take some time and do that now.

What is *logic?* There are two species of logic: formal and informal logic. Of course, throughout western tradition there have been several divisions: deductive and inductive, formal and material, analytic and dialectic, general and transcendental, Aristotelian and symbolic. Aristotle, who Immanuel Kant called the father of logic, enumerated logic, or dialectic, as the art of criticizing or studying the formal components of discourse about anything. That is to say, when we "do logic," we are answering the questions, "Is it? What is it? And why is it?" For Isaac Watts, "Logic is the art of using reason well in our inquiries after truth, and the communication of it to others."[13] John Frame in *The Doctrine of the Christian Life* defines reason as, "Reason, or intellect, is the capacity to make logical inferences and to judge the logical consistency of ideas and behavior."[14] Following right along with *Introductory Logic* by James Nance and Douglas Wilson, logic is the science and art of reasoning well. "Formal logic deals directly with reasoning, by considering the means of distinguishing between proper and improper modes of reasoning. Informal logic deals with operations of thinking that are indirectly related to reasoning, such as defining terms, relating terms to each other, and determining relationships between statements." Thus, logic in the broad sense is something we do by default. God gives this gift to intelligent creatures. By it, we may communicate more effectively, know truth more fully, and love God more faithfully.

Logic is not a product of man's fall, man's depravity. It was there from the foundations of the earth. We reason all the time without even recognizing it. We are often persuaded and persuade others by reasons. Politicians use logic. Teachers use logic. Babies use logic. Criminals use logic. Judges use logic. God uses logic. Some would even say computers use a kind of logic. I am currently relying on logic to write this as are you to read it. Unfortunately, we have a propensity to both persuade and be persuaded by faulty reasoning. For these reasons, the study of logic is a worthwhile endeavor, even a necessary good. The ancients saw such endeavors as being inseparable from our nature as social creatures. Augustine in *On Christian Doctrine*, stated it this way:

"And yet the validity of logical sequences is not a thing devised by men, but is observed and noted by them that they may be able to learn and teach it; for it exists eternally in the reason of things, and has its origin with God. For as the man who narrates the order of events does not himself create that order; and as he who describes the situations of places, or the natures of animals, or roots, or minerals, does not describe arrangements of man; and as he who points out the stars and their movements does not point out anything that he himself or any other man has ordained; in the same way, he who says, 'When the consequent is false, the antecedent must also be false,' says what is most true; but he does not himself make it so, he only points out that it is so."[15]

What is *arguing*? With regards to the application of logic, we find argument at the center. Argument, or disputation, can take many forms. One distinction which must be made is that arguing, or being in an argument, is not the same as *being argumentative*. An argument has great potential to be used to love and serve your neighbor while being argumentative has an intrinsic, belligerent bite to it. One is constructive in and of itself while the other is necessarily destructive. One is done by good men while the other by pessimistic narcissists. In chapter ten of *The Improvement of the Mind*, Watts defines disputing as "...when two or more persons appear to maintain different sentiments, and defend their own, or oppose the other's opinion, in alternate discourse, by some methods of argument." Arguments may take ten seconds to present. They could last several weeks. They could take place between individuals, between groups, or even interpersonally. Technically, "an argument is a set of statements, one of which appears to be implied or supported by the others."[16]

For now, it is important to know and remember that there are two kinds of men who find themselves in a debate: *faithful men* and *unfaithful men*. Unfaithful men are those who have the stench of being dissentious and argumentative. They argue for the sake of personal pride or public renown. The ancient sophists were these kinds of men. Their concern was not for arguing for truth and its benefit to society writ-large. They presented a counterfeit wisdom, or what Aristotle calls, "a wisdom which exists only in semblance." The sophist concern was to fill their own pockets. Watch Congressional debates long enough and you will see that these kinds of public figures do not go away—they have almost convinced me that eastern forms of re-incarnation are possible. Therefore, sophistication is not a mark of godliness, of biblical wisdom. Unfaithful men debate, not for the good of their neighbor and the glory of God, but for their own private, wicked concerns, usually their own renown.

By contrast, there are *faithful men* who debate. Faithful men are the kind who debate in order to seek to know God's truth and make it known. They tend to have a certain posture of deference, humility, and love toward their neighbor. They look for real conclusions. Faithful men are neither perfect nor always right simply because they are faithful. Likewise, unfaithful men are not necessarily wrong simply because they are behaving like Penelope's suitors. As Christians, we should seek to be faithful men in debate.

And we should be ever aware of our deep propensity to be unfaithful with every gift of God, including logic.

What is *street-fighting logic*? Street-fighting logic is the kind of thing that happens all around us. I'm sure many of us are aware of it, but probably call it something else, like "those loud men at the coffee shop" or "cousin Jim's stubborn defiance." Street-fighting logic is your brother fussing with your mom about whether or not he has to clean his room before going to the birthday party. It is your teacher explaining why he chose a certain book to be in the curriculum. It is the police officer pulling over your dad and explaining his driving offense, and your dad explaining to the cop— of course in a gentle and loving tone—why he does not deserve to receive this citation. It is the guy at the coffee shop arguing with his friend whether God really exists. More historically grounded, the street-fighting logician resembles the orator more than he resembles the scientist or dialectician. This is because the ultimate aim of logic as employed by the street-fighting logician is one of identification and persuasion.

I first came across the term in Nance and Wilson's *Introductory Logic* text. The beginning of lesson thirty-three states, "This unit will consider the use and identification of reasoning that, despite their popularity, are invalid or unhelpful. Studying and responding to such casual mistakes make up an important part of what we might call 'street-fighting' logic. In learning 'street-fighting' logic, the first thing to do (as always) is to make some distinctions." To give more of a stipulative definition, street-fighting logic will here refer to the informal application of formal and informal logic to common-place scenarios, whether employed knowingly or unknowingly in conversation and disputation. In short, it is the nitty-gritty, everyday arguments that occur all around us. Most importantly, it is contextual, though informally so. It occurs at a given time, in a particular space and between distinct persons, hardly planned as such. It does not simply involve the abstract or discursive, but involves the passions, the feelings, and the body. It involves the paradoxical. It involves the poetic. It involves the entire human being, who is heart, soul, mind and strength. It is technical, but only as much as human beings are technical, which is to say, not as much as modern anthropology would have us think. It may center on great philosophical issues or life's tremendous trifles. Suffice it to say that nearly every student who ever steps foot into a formal class on logic will be a street-fighting logician for the remainder of their life, and certainly was one before they came to class. That is to say, the vast majority of our students are not and will not become philosophers or logicians in the proper sense.

Street-fighting logic is the kind of thing that should affect us and our opponent emotionally as much as it affects us intellectually. It takes into account the whole person and the world that is at all times surrounding each person. As Wilson says, "Human reasoning takes much of its meaning from context. Informal or 'street-fighting logic' is not as neat or mathematical as formal logic." Thus, street-fighting logic is a kind of *techne*. I use this term in the same way Plato used it in his *Republic*. It is a craft, an art, and in so much as it is an art, it seeks to benefit the person to whom the art is aimed; namely, your opponent. It will be a goal of this present work to sift through some of its mire and sort out how we could be better prepared in season and out of season to artfully debate as faithful men and women. There are always opportunities to engage in street-fighting logic. Walk the aisles of your local grocery store. Turn on the television or radio. Visit the school office. The examples are endless. Those who do it well are not.

What Good is Logic?

Having set some groundwork, why is logic a necessary good within any academic curriculum? And why should Christians desire to argue and work at arguing well? God calls us to love Him with our entire mind. But what does this mean? In his excellent textbook *Socratic Logic*, Peter Kreeft opens the introduction by asking "What good is logic?" He goes on to present thirteen answers to this question, which are worth giving here before I give my own:

1. *Order.* "Logic builds the mental habit of thinking in an orderly way."
2. *Power.* "Logic has power: the power of proof and thus persuasion."
3. *Reading.* "Logic will help you with all your other courses, for logic will help you to read any book more clearly and effectively."
4. *Writing.* "Logic will also help you to write more clearly and effectively, for clear writing and clear thinking are a 'package deal': the presence or absence of either one brings the presence or absence of the other."
5. *Happiness.* "In a small but significant way, logic can even help you attain happiness."
6. *Religious faith.* "All religions require faith...Even religion, though it goes *beyond* logic, cannot go against it...logic can aid faith."
7. *Wisdom.* "*Philosophy* means 'the love of wisdom'. Although logic alone cannot make you wise, it can help. For logic is one of philosophy's main instruments."
8. *Democracy.* "There are even crucial social and political reasons for studying logic."

9. *Defining logic's limits.* "Does logic have limits? Yes, but we need logic to recognize and define logic's limits."
10. *Testing authority.* "We need authority as well as logic. But we need logic to test our authorities."
11. *Recognizing contradictions.* "Logic teaches us which ideas contradict each other."
12. *Certainty.* "Logic has 'outer limits'; there are many things it can't give you. But logic has no 'inner limits': like math, it never breaks down."
13. *Truth.* "Our last reason for studying logic is the simplest and most important of all. It is that logic helps us to find truth, and truth is its own end: it is worth knowing for its own sake."

Vern S. Poythress, professor of New Testament interpretation at Westminster Theological Seminary and copious author on philosophy, literature, and language, makes his own significant mark on a distinctly Christian approach to logic in his *Logic: A God-centered Approach to the Foundation of Western Thought*. Similar to Kreeft, Poythress opens the beginning chapters of his text in an attempt to answer the question "Why Study Logic?" There he provides several answers to this question:

"...we struggle with an apparent conflict between logic and emotion..."
"...some people find logic intrinsically interesting..."
"...others study it for practical purposes..."
"Logic has had a profound influence on the whole of Western thought..."
"...logic has had indirect influence. People engage in reasoning in every area of serious study, not just in philosophy..."

"Logic has also influenced perceptions about the contrast between rationality on the one hand and emotion, desire, and imagination on the other..."

"Arguments can help lead us to a wise conclusion. But they can also lead us astray...

"Arguments occur in the Bible..."

"Arguments can be used to deceive and manipulate..."[17]

Both authors' reasons, Kreeft's thirteen points and Poythress's several, can be condensed to four broader principles showing why studying logic is a necessary good within any learning environment:

1. Studying logic is a necessary good within any learning environment because God reasons well and commands we do the same. Since logic primarily deals with the pursuit of truth, since God is the God of truth, since God wants us to know and discern truth, and since God told us to reason wisely, then Christians should care about logic. Both the Old Testament and the New Testament are saturated with this kind of God who wants this kind of people. Spend some time looking up the following passages. Allow them to begin constructing for you a biblical foundation for understanding logic: 1 Samuel 23:11-13, Job 37:16, 1 John 3:20, Titus 1:2, Matthew 22:37-39, I Peter 3:14-15, John 17:17, Isaiah 1:18 , Acts 4, Acts 17:17, Acts 26, Romans 12:1-2, Ecclesiastes 6:10, Jeremiah 12:1, Jeremiah 20:12

2. Studying logic is a necessary good within any learning environment because reasoning has played an important role in defining the Christian Church throughout history. Early in our studies of the New Testament, we find men and women with great intellectual abilities. Some of the verses above can attest to that. However, the use of the mind was not confined to the first century. Even in the first generation after the New Testament writers and onward to today, Christian literature is littered not with intellectual slouches but with authors of pastoral and polemical treatises who defend, define, and decorate the Christian faith in all its rightful glory. From the Church fathers into our own time, the reasoning faculty within man has been both explored and employed for offensive and defensive purposes. The Church throughout history has combined proper reasoning with Scriptural revelation to provide future Christians with doctrinal boundaries and practical application of those doctrines. The following quotes are just a few morsels from a greater buffet:

St. Thomas Aquinas (1225 – 1274):
"Now Scripture inspired of God is not part of the philosophical sciences, which have been built up by human reason. Therefore it is useful that besides philosophical doctrine there should be other knowledge that is, inspired of God. I answer that, it was necessary for man's salvation that there should be a knowledge revealed by God, besides the philosophical sciences built up by human reason."[18]

John Calvin (1509 - 1564):
"...the more anyone endeavors to approach to God, the more he proves himself endowed with reason."[19]

John Wesley (1703 – 1791):
"Ought not a Minister to have, First, a good understanding, a clear apprehension, a sound judgment, and a capacity of reasoning with some closeness?"[20]

James Orr (1844 – 1913):
"If there is a religion in the world which exalts the office of teaching, it is safe to say that it is the religion of Jesus Christ...A religion divorced from earnest and lofty thought has always, down the whole history of the Church, tended to become weak, jejune and unwholesome, while the intellect, deprived of its rights within religion, has sought its satisfaction without, and developed into a godless rationalism."[21]

G.K. Chesterton (1874 - 1936)
"The general fact is simple. Poetry is sane because it floats easily in an infinite sea; reason seeks to cross the infinite sea, and so make it finite...The poet only asks to get his head into the heavens. It is the logician who seeks to get the heavens into his head. And it is his head that splits."[22]

C.S. Lewis (1898 – 1963):
"He [Christ] wants a child's heart, but a grown-up's head."[23]

3. Studying logic is a necessary good within any learning environment because studying logic matures our brains and our being. There is no subject in the world, not one, which exists apart from logic. As Peter Kreeft states, "No course is more practical than logic, for no matter what you are thinking *about*, you are *thinking*, and logic orders and clarifies your thinking...The principles of thinking logically can be applied to *all* thinking and to every field."[24] Any vocation you pursue, any task you are employed to fulfill, any country you visit, any language you try to speak, will all in some way build upon a foundation of proper reasoning. Of course, there are basic beliefs, as alluded to above, which need neither inductive nor deductive reasoning in order to hold. Still, as rational creatures, we have a distinctly close relationship with the intellectual mode of reasoning. As Watts states in the introduction to his treatise on logic, "In so polite and knowing an age, every man of reason will covet some acquaintance with logic, since it renders its daily service to wisdom and virtue, and to the affairs of common life, as well as to the sciences."[25]

Logic is not just a Christian way of knowing the Christian God and his revelation of himself in both his world and his Word. Logic was used by the ancient pagans (i.e. Socrates, Plato, Aristotle, Isocrates, Quintilian, Cicero, *et cetera*). In a purely psychological and humanistic sense, the study of logic really can make you think faster and more cogently. The simple process of learning to reason well can help you better learn and participate in other endeavors, like politics, theology, philosophy, or horseriding. As has been said elsewhere, the more you know, the more you can know. And certainly, logic is the kind of gift which can increase our understanding and knowledge of both God's Word and his world, despite our theological confession.

In running an ACT prep company, I come across all kinds of students, and the distinguishing factor between those who can take the test better than others are two-fold: reading and reasoning. While I do not support pragmatic, secular humanistic arguments, the argument for logic holds even in this area. The following quotes are worth perusing:

Aristotle (384–322 B.C.)
"The animals other than man live by appearances and memories, and have but little of connected experience; but the human race also lives by art and reasonings."[26]

Cicero (106-43 B.C.)

"So evidently Archytas rightly looked on anger (that is, when it was at variance with his judgment) as a kind of revolt within the mind, and he was anxious to quell it by rational reflection. Bring in greed, bring in lust, bring in the desire for power and glory; then you realize that if there is to be a ruling power in the human mind, it will be the sovereignty of a single element, namely reason (for that is the best part of the mind). A long as reason is supreme there is no room for lust, anger, or irresponsible behavior."[27]

Epictetus (about 60 A.D. - 110)

" You are not going to tell me, are you, that setting fire to the Capitol and killing one's father are the only forms of wrong-doing? To deal with one's impressions without thought or method, to fail to follow argument or demonstration or sophism, in a word, to be unable to see what concerns himself and what does not in question and answer – is there no wrongdoing, I ask, in any of these?" [28]

Petrarch (1304 - 1374)

"...I know well in what esteem it was held by that sturdy and virile sect of philosophers, the Stoics, whom our Cicero frequently mentions, especially in his work De Finibus. I know that it is one of the liberal studies, a ladder for those who are striving upwards, and by no means a useless protection to those who are forcing their way through the thorny thickets of philosophy. It stimulates the intellect, points out the way of truth, shows us how to avoid fallacies, and finally, if it accomplishes nothing else, makes us ready and quick-witted. All this I readily admit, but because a road is proper for us to traverse, it does not immediately follow that we should linger on it forever." [29]

Georg Wilhelm Friedrich Hegel (1770-1831)
"Logic has a utility value. It produces a cultivated mind. Man matures in his practice of thought, and in his reflection upon it. Utility, however, is not the highest value of logic. The term "logical" is equivalent to "trustful"; logic is truth in the form of truth."[30]

Peter Kreeft (1937 – Present)
"Logic builds the mental habit of thinking in an orderly way. A course in logic will do this for you even if you forget every detail in it (which you won't, by the way), just as learning Latin will make you more habitually aware of the structure of language even if you forget every particular Latin word and rule." [31]

4. Studying logic is a necessary good within any learning environment because studying logic matures our souls and the souls of others. To truly reason well, we cannot simply learn rules and plug them in. Contrary to what has been posited since the Industrial and Scientific Revolutions, man is not merely a collection of mechanical parts. When we reason well, we reason soundly. And when we reason soundly, we also come to accurately know truth, goodness, and beauty. This participation in the knowledge of truth, goodness, and beauty is something that should do two things. First, it should grant us a better understanding of who we are. Exercising our reason will not only show how capable we are as humans at a number of great endeavors, but also how weak and frail we are at an innumerable amount of others. Through logic, we not only come to defy gravity and kick moon rocks, we also realize our inclination to use logic, like all other gifts God gives us, for evil ends. In so doing this, we begin to realize our place in the universe, and our propensity to extend ourselves to places we do not belong, like the realm of acting as the ultimate authority for our own lives.

Second, accurately knowing truth, goodness, and beauty always means moving toward or into a right relationship with other persons: a more accurate understanding of the Triune God and our neighbor, which in turn should lead to a more complete worship of that Triune God and a healthier interaction in earthly communities. Logic unfolds truths that always were and always will be. In the introduction to his treatise on logic, Watts writes to his friend of the reason for beginning and finishing such a work. He states, "I have therefore collected and proposed the chief principles and sacred importance, and pointed out our most frequent mistakes and prejudices in the concerns of life and religion, that we might better guard against the springs of error, guilt and sorrow, which surrounds us in our state of mortality."[32] This "guarding against the springs of error" is an endeavor which plays out in a social setting, which has social implications for good.

As Watts goes on to say, "Now the design of logic is to teach us the right use of our reason, or intellectual powers, and the improvement of them in ourselves and others: this is not only necessary in order to attain any competent knowledge in the sciences, or the affairs of learning, but to govern both the greater and the meaner actions of life. It is the cultivation of our reason by which we are better enabled to distinguish good from evil, as well as truth from falsehood: and both of these are matters of the highest importance, whether we regard this life, or the life to come."[33] In short, Watts rightly sees little separation between the ethics a society lives or dies by and the proper use of logic. Likewise, our reasoning faculties should be strengthened because *veritas in puteo*, 'Truth lives in a well'. Because of this, logic has been used by the ancients, and can be used by us modern folks, to draw the truth out of the well that we may drink, and offer a large gulp to our neighbor.[34]

Truth is often not as apparent as we may think, especially given that we are fallen creatures whose sin has a great tendency to misinterpret and pervert the world around us, or whose sin or genuine ignorance of others, either those in authority over us or our peers, leads us into lies and deceit. As Aleksander Solzhenitsyn began his 1978 commencement address to Harvard's graduating class,

"Harvard's motto is 'Veritas.' Many of you have already found out and others will find out in the course of their lives that truth eludes us if we do not concentrate with total attention on its pursuit. And even while it eludes us, the illusion still lingers of knowing it and leads to many misunderstandings. Also, truth is seldom pleasant; it is almost invariably bitter."

Even through our foggy search and apprehension of truth, as Romans 1 tells us, we have been plainly shown the invisible attributes of God through the visible world. With this revelation, we are without excuse to both know and worship God. We are also not without explanation as to why every human has a propensity to seek the happy life. God has so given us the gift of logic to aid in this endeavor: to promote the process of conversion, sanctification, mortification of sin, and fulfillment of the command to love him with our minds. Augustine stated it this way, "For if I put the question to anyone whether he prefers to find joy in the truth or in falsehood, he does not hesitate to say that he prefers the truth, just as he does not hesitate to say he wants to be happy. The happy life is joy based on the truth. This joy is grounded in you, O God, who are the truth....This happy life everyone desires; joy in the truth everyone wants." [35]

A Christian Epistemology

The popular need for a proper understanding and use of logic is simply a more specific need which has come about because of a broader problem: we as Christians have not maintained or lived by a distinctly Christian epistemology. Epistemology is the branch of philosophy which answers the questions, "What do we know? How do we know it? What can we know? How can we know it? What does it matter?" Christian epistemology is not somehow a different species of epistemology. Christian epistemology is a view of knowledge according to Scripture and Christian Church history. And if Scripture and Church history are correct, then Christian epistemology is how the world actually works; it is the only accurate posture we could have toward a theory of knowledge. *Christian epistemology, therefore, is epistemological realism.*

This particular need—for Christians to have and live by a distinctly Christian epistemology—is most apparent in Christian schools. When Christians differ on education, they differ further down. They differ in the foundations. Epistemology is a foundational issue. What can we know? How can we know it? And what does it matter? The broad sentiment spoken of earlier, the fact-value split, has been adopted by a vast number of Christians. Christians—because of the lack of a distinctly Christian epistemology and because the Lordship of Christ has not been seen as comprehensive over all human realms – have adopted the lie that some truths are public and some are private. The public and the private, so the argument goes, must be kept separate. The 'public truths' are called 'facts'. The 'private truths' are called 'opinions'. And the public always trumps the private: God's economy has nothing to do with our nation's financial crisis; English literature can—and should—be taught without reference to the Bible; one may have faith or science, but not both; an education at a non-

Christian school does not negatively affect a student's worldview; religion and politics are kept separate. In believing these, we all fall to our death down the dark, confused chasm which separates the Church and the State. Not only are these false dichotomies, they are ultimately a mockery of the Triune God's character, work, and revelation. Because of the basic doctrines which define a distinctly Christian theology and sociology, those who profess Christ ought to have a particular view of how we get knowledge and what we do with the knowledge revealed to us by our Creator and Sustainer.

Because the two branches of epistemology are *logic* (the art and science of reasoning well) and *rhetoric* (the art and science of a good man speaking well), it is imperative we have a proper view of logic in order to have a proper view of epistemology. Without turning this present work into a *magnus opus* for Christian epistemology, a distinctly Christian view of knowledge should uphold these thirteen qualifications:

- *Fear is the beginning.* Fear of the Lord is foundational for any lasting epistemology. "The fear of the Lord is the beginning of knowledge; fools despise wisdom and instruction." (Prov. 1:7) [36] When seeking to gain knowledge from reading or listening to Scripture, we are instructed by Augustine that, "After these two stages of fear and holiness comes the third stage, that of knowledge..." [37] This goes for all lasting knowledge whatsoever.

- *Truth exists.* Man can and should make truth claims. Man should also live by those truth claims, simultaneously rejecting any statement which contradicts them. Man should be able to locate nonsense, such as the Liar's Paradox. "There is no truth" is an example of the Liar's Paradox. "This statement is false" and "Obey no command" are other examples.

• *Man is finite.* Man cannot know all truth. While man can know something truly and accurately, there is nothing he fully knows.

• *Man is broken.* Man's relationship to truth is broken. Man's ability to comprehend and live by the truth is corrupted by sin. Though we may know truth propositionally, our hearts may not obey it. We may reject the truth, while also knowing it is true. Likewise, our broken state warps our understanding some of the most basic truth-claims. Not only do we not do what we *ought to do* (sins of omission), we reason to doing what we *ought not do* (sins of commission). As John Frame says, "…reason is not infallible. Sometimes it guides us wrongly. Sin infects our reasoning, as Paul teaches in Romans 1 and in 1 Corinthians 2:14. There is an antithesis between the wisdom of God and the wisdom of the world. So even though we are obligated to obey reason, we sometimes sin when we do so." [38]

• *Logic is good.* It is good to reason well. Though broken, our reasoning faculty can be redeemed and is reliable. The most heinous man in the world can have valid arguments to support his actions. And he may very well base his actions on the validity of those arguments. He is not wrong for reasoning. He is wrong for using a gift like logic for ill-gain. He is likewise wrong for the evil he commits whether he reasons validly to those evils or not. Again, Frame is helpful. "Like conscience and experience, reason requires God's grace to function rightly. God made our reason to function rightly only on the presupposition of the truth of his word. The authority of God's revelation is the highest of the laws of thought. By saving grace in Christ, God enables us to think according to that revelation." [39]

◦ *All reason requires faith.* Faith and reason are not opposing acts. All acts of the intellect require faith. Any truth-claim whatsoever requires faith. It requires, at some point, submission to an authority which cannot be empirically proven. It requires a conviction of things we cannot see. Chesterton said it best: "It is idle to talk always of the alternative of reason and faith. Reason is itself a matter of faith. It is an act of faith to assert that our thoughts have any relation to reality at all." [40]

• *Natural revelation matters.* A non-Christian can know truth. There is *natural revelation.* It is called *natural* because it is possible for all people. It is called *revelation* because no man can know the truth without God's grace. Justin Martyr reminds us, "And whatever both philosophers and poets have said concerning the immortality of the soul, or punishments after death, or contemplation of things heavenly, or doctrines of the like kind, they have received such suggestions from the prophets as have enabled them to understand and interpret these things. And hence there seem to be seeds of truth among all men." [41] Thomas in his *Summa* handles the topic similarly. "As the knowledge of God's essence is by grace, it belongs only to the good, but the knowledge of Him by natural reason can belong to both good and bad; and hence Augustine says…'For it can be answered that many who are not pure can know many truths,' that is, by natural reason." [42] More than any Church father, Augustine was the most notorious for coining the idea of 'plundering the Egyptians.' He states, "A person who is a good and a true Christian should realize that truth belongs to his Lord, wherever it is found, gathering and acknowledging it even in pagan literature, but rejecting superstitious vanities…" [43]

* *Special revelation matters.* There is some knowledge only revealed by God to his Church. It is a particular or special grace given to God's people for God's good purposes. It is revealed to us primarily in the Scriptures, in the person of Christ, and by the ministry of the Holy Spirit. This is quite an anti-rationalistic sentiment; it does not square with the idea that man can, with only a bit more brains and brawn, figure everything out, or at least figure it out truly and accurately. Man cannot find God by being more clever at it. By *natural revelation*, man comes to know what is true and what is not. By *special revelation*, man comes to have the saving knowledge that truth, goodness, and beauty reside in the Triune God.

* *Being is sacramental.* All creation participates in the Being of God and likewise effectually provides a kind of array of signs (*signum*) pointing toward and participating in a greater reality (*res*), the Signified. Traditionally this is called *sacramental ontology*. As Hans Boersma explains, "A sacramental ontology insists that not only does the created world point to God as its source and 'point of reference,' but that it also subsists or participates in God…because creation is a sharing in the being of God, our connection with God is a *participatory*, or real, connection – not just an *external*, or nominal, connection." [44] The epistemological implications here are enormous. Within the framework of sacramental ontology, all knowledge therefore is for *enjoyment* before it is for *use*. This distinction between enjoyment and use is important in the German Catholic philosopher Josef Pieper's distinction between work and leisure. It also means that all knowledge is inherently mysterious, ultimately incomprehensible to us. As Boersma clarifies, "….though our hands, eyes, ears, nose, and tongues are able to access reality, they cannot *fully* grasp this reality. They cannot *comprehend* it. The reason for this basic incomprehensibility of the universe was that

the world was, as the poet Gerard Manley Hopkins famously put it, 'charged with the grandeur of God.' " [45]

• *Rationalism is bankrupt.* Man's pursuit of truth via pure reason ends tragically. This has been properly called *secular humanism.* This is a view of man *qua* man which places man's faculties, particularly rationality, at the center. Man via reason becomes the sole authority for determining truth. Given number four above—that man is broken—rationalism is the worst form of slavery: *self-slavery.*

• *Knowledge is incarnational.* Our bodies are essential to our understanding. Bodies are not accidentals, and the body does not corrupt the intellect merely because one is material and the other is not. Pure intellect with no corporeal interchange cannot exist among humans. As Thomas states, "…the use of reason depends in a certain manner on the use of the sensitive powers." [46] In order to reason properly, our bodies must be functioning well enough in the world to act as a basis for our reasoning faculties. Likewise, for humans, all reasoning takes place in the context of flesh and bone, of space, shade, shadow, and climates of all kinds. Life is always life in the lived-body. John Frame states, "…perception is dependent on reason." [47] Surely the reverse is true: reason is dependent on perception. As Frame goes onto say, "Reason cannot accomplish anything unless it has an object – something to reason about. For example, there can be no moral syllogism without premises. And those premises require sensory knowledge; they cannot be derived from reason or logic alone. There can be no reasoning about means and ends without situations to analyze. There be no reasoning about Scripture without Scripture." [48] In this way, *incarnational humanism* is a legitimate kind of humanism for Christians. Norman Klassen and Jens Zimmermann say it well in *The Passionate Intellect:*

Incarnational Humanism and the Future of University Education.
They are worth quoting at length:

> "We are not individuals but persons. To be human is not to be
> a reflective consciousness but a person in relation…Reason is
> our ability to reflect on our existence; reason, however, is not a
> mere intellectual activity that promises direct and pure access to
> complete truth – such is the privilege of God. But even God is
> not pure reason; God, particularly in the Judeo-Christian
> tradition is relational through and through. Reason is primarily
> the means by which we know that we do not know everything
> and the means by which we enjoy our world. It includes our
> emotions. It never stands alone and is not the cool center of our
> being apart from our emotions, apart from other or from the
> past. Rational reflection depends on personal motives and
> cultural and educational influences. Reason is not a set of ready-
> made assumptions about or interpretations of reality that
> somehow float unchangingly and eternally in the heavens, just
> waiting to be discovered. Instead reason is our reflective ability
> and our rational interpretations of reality as shaped by the books
> we read, the people we grow up with, the culture we live in, the
> language(s) we speak, the things we do. To think rationally is
> already to think in dialogue with other human beings and with
> traditions that are older and greater than yourselves. Reason is
> not beholden to politics, and yet it is inescapably political. It is
> potentially universal, although its unfolding character means
> that we never have complete clarity as individuals or collectively.
> Toleration is always required. And humility. They always will
> be." [49]

- *Truth is a Person.* "I am the way, the truth, and the life. No one comes to the Father except through me." (John 14:6) Truth is ultimately found in a Person, and not in man's self-driven attempt to adhere to all the correct propositions in the universe. Because truth is a Person, truth is both revelatory and relational. We cannot know or apply the truth outside of community. It is distinctly relational. It is self-given. It is not so much that we find truth. Truth finds us.

- *Worship is the goal.* To worship the Triune God in spirit and truth is the goal of knowing anything whatsoever. Knowing truth is awe-ful, in that it is full of awe; truth leads us to praise something. We will give thanks somewhere. Odysseus thanked the bright-eyed goddess. The naturalist thanks Mother Earth. The secular scientist thanks reason and chance, his own twisted aptitude, maybe the dead guys who helped him get here, and certainly our worthy primate ancestors who sacrificed so much in evolution's lottery.

A Christian epistemology likewise sees the laws of logic as comprehensive, universally relevant. There is a deep reasonableness which governs all human thinking. And that reasonableness is the same regardless of religion, gender, age, nationality, political affiliations, or vocation. Have you ever heard someone say a sentence which is preceded by a "So…" or "Therefore…"? Have you ever heard your parents say "Because I said so" or heard a news reporter say something to the effect of "That doesn't make any sense."? These phrases carry an aroma of reasoning. As is learned from studying syllogisms, some of these words are 'buzz-words' which give clues to where the conclusion of the argument is located. Search the teleprompter before. Ask your parents what they were thinking before that phrase and you will find an argument. It might be a scattered, unsound non-sequitur. But it is there. And it is now the reason why you cannot go to your friend's party, or why hundreds of viewers of the five o'clock news just decided to not vote for that Presidential candidate. They are called the *laws* of logic because they are not suggestions for just one man or one people group on earth. They are laws put forth by the reality in which we live. This reality speaks to us about how we *ought* to live.

Logic transcends cultures. It transcends situations. It transcends worldviews and religions. If you have not already caught it, it should be said again: *logic is one of the most basic elements of human existence.* We live in a reality which necessitates that we both make truth claims and act according to those truth claims. It also necessitates that we can rightly evaluate those truth claims as agreeable or disagreeable, true or false, reliable or unreliable. To do otherwise would quickly lead to constant error, perpetual confusion, and a quick death. It would be like living in a world where language had no form or rules of engagement. All would be nonsense, nihilism. Without logic I could write, but hardly defend, *"veritas* I si Aristotle supports Rap!hael and *Donec Requiscat in Te".* Got it? Good. Thus, it is wise to think logically. Bad arguments are no mark of a faithful Christian or a respectable civilization.

It makes no difference whether Western tradition has sheered more sheep or cut down more trees in order to refine the subject of both informal and formal logic while the Asian east has been able to successfully ignore any substantial tomes on the subject. A man arguing in a Chinese marketplace is just as accountable to the laws of logic as the major league baseball coach who runs onto the multi-million dollar blades of grass to emphatically explain why his player was safe. Both are susceptible to the consequences for breaking these same, transcendent laws, and both are surrounded by bugs who could care less whether they eat sod from underneath Derek

Jeter's cleat or wild oats from the ancestral fields of the Yen Dynasty. Like any law – divine, moral, judicial, mathematical, or natural – laws of logic can be disobeyed. And, like any law, disobedience carries with it consequences. Sometimes the consequences can be as small as being swindled out of five dollars. Other times the consequences can be substantial, like seeing evil as a problem and then illogically reasoning that an omnipotent, all-loving God cannot *therefore* exist.

Logic only matters if there is a purpose to the world. It makes the most sense in the Christian metanarrative. *A Christian epistemology is therefore the only epistemology worth having.* An atheistic epistemology, for example, is a contradiction in theory and practice. A pantheistic epistemology cannot be obeyed with any regularity. If the world has no ultimate purpose and our lives are only as valuable as the cranberry gelatin your grandmother plopped onto the holiday saucer last Thanksgiving, then there is no need to read any further. Put the book down. Step away from the pages. I'm sure network television has something to offer us. Logic only matters if our actions matter, if our thoughts matter. Ultimately, logic is not about good ideas and elaborate theories. Logic is more materialistic than that. Logic loves the earth and all the material transformations more than we do. Logic only matters as much as our practical life upon earth matters. And because our practice on earth matters a great deal—I would argue that our practice on earth has eternal consequences—so logic is something which we cannot afford to ignore. We ought not to live as if logic is merely an accident of being human. In this way, logic cares deeply about the ethical and political reality in which we live and the consequences of those realities which extend beyond our own time.

Logic as a necessary good and an imminent need in our place as humans cannot be overstated. It could be misstated, but it could not be overstated. As it turns out, the employment of logic in everyday settings is as much of a 'heart' issue as it is a 'head' issue. Our inability to properly reason in both formal and informal settings is not only a symptom of not being properly equipped to do so, it is also a symptom of our desire to fill our time with other endeavors, superficial talk, and surface relationships. The effect, just as well, is one which gets at the heart of our ability as humans to discern the beautiful and the fitting from the detrimental and repulsive, to make wise decisions for the good of the whole, and to act in accordance with the consistent story of a logical Author.

If we love mindless and nonsensical things, things which are simply *amusing*, we will turn into mindless and nonsensical things. Likewise, it is a hideous delight for us to seek self-expression. We should most desire to plod through and traverse the depths of expressing truth. Thankfully, logic is a tool by which we may do just that. Logic is not about self-expression. It is about expressing truth. It is about thinking God's own thoughts after him. As Joel McDurmon states in *Biblical Logic, in Theory and Practice*, "Truth may exist while people reject it; and people may in turn create all types of falsehoods and call them truth. These activities represent fallen man's desperate attempts to impute his own truth instead of God's." [50] If we love a God who is orderly, reasonable, personable, incarnate, and loving, we will bear his image more fully. We will intelligently participate in an intelligible conversation which has not only taken place among men throughout the ages, but is taking place right now, as you read these strategically ordered ink blobs.

The need to understand logic in the classroom, on the white-board, as well as in the market-place, at the dinner table, on the blog-roll, at the coffee shop, among the priests, around the pagans, by the roadside, atop Hollywood, inside the Oval Office, along the lockers at school, and throughout the pages of your favorite book, is inescapable. Ignoring it does not cause its irrelevance. It only increases ours. We are said to live in the Information Age, and I do not doubt that. It is everywhere. However, it has always been everywhere. Information has always surrounded man. What is peculiar about our time is information is able to be circulated faster and in a thousand different media at once. And can you believe that we are trying to get faster modes of communication and larger operating systems? Yet, we have neither changed in our propensity to be reactionary nor in the amount of time it takes for the earth to make her single rotation, creating light to see and darkness to sleep. We are simply able to promulgate the mass of information at a faster rate and with greater enthusiasm. What is most peculiar to our time is that we do not take the time to synthesize and question the information we receive. We fly through flashing lights and rows of advertisements which reach for our souls without a due penetration into their meaning or the consequences thereof.

Too many people today leave conversations indifferent, scratching their chin and saying, "Well, that's interesting." God calls us to affirm or deny. We are called to affirm truth and deny falsity. To do either, we must have a reliable method and ability to both affirm and deny. Society necessitates this. We function best when our *yes* is *yes* and our *no* is *no*, when a statement cannot be both true and false at the same time and the same respect. Community requires this kind of interaction between its participants. And it requires that we are consistent in our affirmations and denials, which becomes the basis of integrity and trust. Politicians who flip-flop on policies, especially contradictory policies, leave the public confused and bitter, and rightfully so. They prove themselves either spineless worms who cannot take a stand for anything or those with very poor reasoning skills – the high probability of both being true is not off the table. With citizens who think well, these public officials will not long remain in office, even if the official voted 'yes' 45 times and 'no' 42 times on the issue. Both 'yes' citizens and 'no' citizens will throw his lukewarm, pinstriped sentiments to the curb.

Finally, just as there are two kinds of men who get into an argument, it has remained true that there are two ways to live in this carnival we call life: faithfully and unfaithfully. The difference between the two is how we handle words, particularly the Word. If we are to live the former, as the faithful, we must recover our love for and ability to employ logic as faithfully as possible. As Watts reminds us, "Our wisdom, prudence and piety, our present conduct, and our future hope, are all influenced by the use of our rational powers in the search after truth." [51] If we are to live as the latter, as the unfaithful, we are to confuse, conflate and contradict words as often as possible. And as Screwtape reminds us, this is not a difficult trick for humans to learn.

Focus Questions.

1. What are the four reasons why learning logic is a necessary good?
2. What is street-fighting logic?
3. What is the difference between an argument, a debate, and a quarrel?
4. What is Christian epistemology and why is it important?
5. Does sin affect our reasoning ability? If so, how?
6. Of the thirteen reasons Peter Kreeft gives us to study logic, which one do you think is the most important? Why?

Exercises.

1. How many middle schools and high schools are in your city? What percentage of those schools teach at least one formal year of a logic course? Contact a few of those schools and see if they would explain why they do or do not offer a logic class.
2. Find and list five examples from your personal experience where people have used street-fighting logic in an attempt to persuade.
3. Ask one parent, your pastor, and a stranger what logic is and if it is important. Why or why not? Record their answers.
4. Read the Bible passages at the beginning of this chapter. Choose your favorite one and memorize it.

Chapter 2

The Training

"So the man who really loves God, who is working under the Lordship of Christ, could write his poetry, compose his music, construct his musical instruments, fashion his statues, paint his pictures, even if no man ever saw them." Francis Schaeffer [52]

"Be not so weak as to imagine, that a life of learning is a life of laziness and ease... *Labor ipse voluptas*" Isaac Watts[53]

"Your man has been accustomed, ever since he was a boy, to have a dozen incompatible philosophies dancing about together inside his head...Jargon, not argument, is your best ally in keeping him from the Church." C.S. Lewis [54]

"A man can't be always defending the truth; there must be a time to feed on it." C.S. Lewis [55]

What serious athlete enters a competition without having done some sort of training, usually a kind of training that puts the Spartans to shame? Often times an athlete in training has a strict diet, buys special clothes, and if he is not a professional athlete he might even quit his day job or take time off in order to prepare for the big competition. This is understandable. Excellence requires time. It demands devotion. And nearly every endeavor in life requires some sort of training time. Even Jesus, before his earthly ministry, retreated to the wilderness for a time in order to better prepare himself for the work ahead. This is healthy. It is good. Premature involvement in certain things can often lead to a perpetual immaturity or, even worse, irrecoverable injuries.

In life there are seasons. Some are seasons of preparation which prepare us for other seasons. When we were babies, we crawled. And we crawled, not because we were going to always be a crawler, but because we were in the first stages of learning to walk. This is one reason why we enroll in school in the early years, and even in the later years. In being faithful with our schoolwork, we are doing the work the Lord *now* has for us so we are prepared for the work the Lord *will have* for us in the future. In learning at a classical Christian institution, a student is encouraged and given the tools to think, act, and speak like a faithful Christian. As young Christians, we watch older men and women, being trained in "the way you should go so that you do not depart from it." (Prov. 22:6) It would be premature to send our students into the world as they currently are and expect them to be salt and light when they are barely salty and lighty themselves. The same principles apply to music, athletics, economics, and combat.

The art of argument requires the same training mentality. In order to argue well, we must be formed and trained in so doing. So, other than having some good, formal courses of logic under our belts, what are some other ways to prepare for employing street-fighting logic? Other than head knowledge of formal and informal logic, what other ways should Christians prepare to use logic in everyday encounters? As was said before, the right use of logic consists of much more than passing a few classes. And, if anything, passing of a few logic classes is not the culmination of one's training in logic, but the beginning. The necessary training required for any student of logic to excel is simple, but it is work. Still, it is rewarding. Below are five important exercises we should build into our weekly, even daily, schedules.

1. Pray. For those of us who have grown up in a Christian environment, it might sound cliché. But in all reality, prayer is the most fundamental exercise to a Christian's everyday practice of logic, and much else for that matter. Given that we are finite creatures who often think we have more control over this wild world than we actually do, prayer is one of the most basic ways we render to God what is rightfully his and remind ourselves of deep truths. What belongs more to God than our words, and words in general? In a way, prayer is a lens-shifter, calibrating our heart to think about and interpret this spoken world rightly. This is one reason why our academy starts each class day with good prayers. It is a reminder. It is an offering. It is a cornerstone to treating our study as worship.

First, prayer is where we affirm to God what the Scriptures say of him. Some call this adoration. Others call it 'agreement'. Either way, it is where we pray back to God the attributes which only he perfectly exhibits. This kind of prayer reminds us of our place before the Almighty Creator. It exalts his grandeur and lifts our eyes upward toward something greater than ourselves.

Second, it would naturally follow that once our eyes have been lifted higher than ourselves, we realize our lowly state. What comes from this realization should be a hearty confession, the kind which affirms in us what is true: that we are sinful by nature, rebellious in thought, word, and deed, and have not lived as we ought in what we have done and what we have failed to do.

Third, we must not remain in appraising our fallen state, but must be moved to realize the great redemption that the Lord has wrought through Jesus Christ and by the Holy Spirit. Here, we cannot help offering up prayers of thanksgiving. The salvation and reconciliation which God is working upon the earth is not just one of 'churchey' type things. Redemption permeates all areas of life: how we eat, what we eat, what we sing, how we sing, our friends, our school work, and our ability to argue with our neighbor. Redemption is pervasive. It is effectual. It spreads and does not leave any part of our lives untouched, as far as the curse is found. Thus, we may here give thanks for that which seems mundane—seeing color—and that which seems unbelievable—accurately knowing God.

Fourth, we have the great privilege of bringing our requests before God. Through prayer and thanksgiving we are able to ask God for a sufficient supply. This we call supplication. We may pray for strength. We may pray for food. We may pray for patience, love, friends, hatred of sin, a mature pastor, or for our grandmother to be healed. Whatever we ask, we are wanting to be supplied by the Triune God, from whom all blessings flow, and for the purpose of turning all supplies and resources back to praise as a living sacrifice; coming full circle where we once again portray a heart of adoration for the one, true God.

So, what does all of this have to do with street-fighting logic? We will touch on this a bit later, but one of the goals of argument is to change people to see the world rightly and act according to God's Word. And we must realize that the only way we are going to change anyone is by the Lord's own doing. This is the very thing Paul was getting at when addressing the church in Corinth.

For when one says, "I follow Paul," and another, "I follow Apollos," are you not being merely human? What then is Apollos? What is Paul? Servants through whom you believed, as the Lord assigned to each. I planted, Apollos watered, but God gave the growth. So neither he who plants nor he who waters is anything, but only God who gives the growth. He who plants and he who waters are one, and each will receive his wages according to his labor. For we are God's fellow workers. You are God's field, God's building. According to the grace of God given to me, like a skilled master builder I laid a foundation, and someone else is building upon it. Let each one take care how he builds upon it. (1 Cor. 3:4-10)

A farmer can toil and till all day long, but if the rains do not come or the birds come in full to pluck the seed from the ground, the farmer has labored in vain. Scripture is littered with the reality that the faithful saints of God who labor and toil must "pray earnestly to the Lord of the harvest to send out laborers into his harvest." (Luke 10:2) As Christians, and especially as Christian scholars, prayer is one of the best ways to protect ourselves from our own conceit and sin, placing our hearts and minds in a proper submission to God. The four kinds of prayer explained above are good places to start. They are not the only way, but a good way. Put these four kinds of prayer together and we have the acronym A.C.T.S. (Adoration, Confession, Thanksgiving, and Supplication). Make these a part of your regular routine of study and argument. Echoing Isaac Watts, "Watch against the pride of your own reason, and a vain conceit of your own intellectual powers, with the neglect of the divine aid and blessing…Offer up therefore, your daily requests to God, the father of lights, that he would bless all your tempts and labours in reading, study, and conversation." [56]

Pastor and author John Piper says, "You will not know what prayer is for until you know that life is war." So, pray often. Pray widely. Pray for friends. Pray for enemies. Pray before you read. Pray after you read. Pray before you argue. Pray after you argue. "Pray without ceasing." (1 Thes. 5:17) All of this is the work of the Christian, especially the one who opens his mouth to convince others of the truth that has found him. Again, Watts reminds us. "He [God] expects to be acknowledged in the common affairs of life; and he does as certainly expect it in the superior operations of the mind, and in the search of knowledge and truth….Christianity so much the more obliges us, by the precepts of Scripture, to invoke the assistance of the true God in all our labours of the mind, for the improvement of ourselves and others…study without prayer is atheism, as well as prayer without study is presumption." [57]

In short, glory belongs to the Lord, especially in argumentation. One's prayer life should reflect that. So, come up with your own prayer. Find Bible verses to pray. When adoring through prayer, affirm the beauty of Christ as the Word, the Logos. When confessing through prayer, admit your proneness to use logic for selfish gain. When thanksgiving through prayer, show gratitude for the privilege to repent from sin and mature in holy love. When supplicating through prayer, request that wisdom be with you to know when to speak and know when not to speak. Tailor the prayer to fit individual situations of argument, whether with your mom or your non-Christian uncle. Memorize the prayer you write. The two prayers below might be of some inspiration to your own creation.

Bishop H.G.C. Moule
"Lord and Savior, true and kind,
Be the master of my mind;
Bless and guide and strengthen still
All my powers of thought and will.
While I ply the scholar's task,
Jesus Christ be near, I ask;
Help the memory, clear the brain,
Knowledge still to seek and gain."

The Christian Scholar's Prayer by Brian Daigle
Our Father in Christ,
In *listening*, make my countenance soft and my reception shrewd.
Fix my attention upon the speaker that they may catch a glimpse of how You attend to both our prayers and ramblings. Teach me to affirm what is right and graciously deny what is false.
May the light of friendship be seen wherever dialogue is found. And cause me to seek to understand before being understood.

In *reading*, make my soul and surroundings the solitude I need for broad comprehension and deep contemplation.

Fix in me wisdom when selecting readings, knowing my time on earth is short.

Teach me steadfast diligence in completion, or peace to put a book aside.

May the light of my reactions be as if the writer were there with me, incarnate.

And cause me to make holy applications according to your Scriptures, Oh Lord.

In *writing*, make my hands conform both craft and content to your goodness.

Fix my arguments in both soundness and relevance.

Teach me metaphors most effective.

May the light of our creatureliness be seen in our own creations.

And cause in me a greater trust of your Spirit's work over my own eloquence

In *thinking*, make my contemplation worthwhile.

Fix my thoughts within earthly bounds, where you have placed us.

Teach me hope, that the lies of the evil one would not take root.

May the light of prudence and purity abound.

And cause in me a love of stillness, that I would know You are God.

In *speaking*, make my being know the weightiness of the tongue, as fire, sword, and healing agent.

Fix my words with great care for the listener.

Teach me when to speak and especially when not to speak.

May the light of wisdom and redemption flow forth to the hearers.

And cause in me a Christian's mouth, that the world would know you are the *Logos.*

When *interruptions* come, however large or small, commit to my being a joyful trust and patience, not in my own strivings, but in Yours.

And in all these, make my heart, soul, mind, and strength wholly submit to the guiding of your Holy Spirit, who has proceeded from the Father and the Son to till the entirety of the saint; that your bride, the church, would be presented to You clean and unblemished according to your holiness, Oh Lord. Amen.

2. Know. The second important aspect of training is to know what you are talking about *before* you start talking. This will closely intertwine and lead to the three aspects of training yet to be explained, but it should be mentioned on its own. It is a great temptation of students who have taken a few respectable classes to want to speak into any situation. It is often the freshman in college who has taken an Introductory to Philosophy course who is found in the lunch room arguing up a storm on a topic of which he knows little. He is equivalent to a babbling child whose lips are loose yet knows not enough to speak intelligently. Do not be that person. I'm not saying a person must know everything about anything before he says something. But one's demeanor in speaking must be relative to what one knows of the topic. If you know little, speak little and ask much. If you know much, humbly share, and seek to know more.

We should begin in great humility, knowing how little we know, even of the topic we know the most about. Try this. Spend as long as you need writing down all you know about the topic with which you are most familiar. Consider how much more of that topic you have yet to discover. Then, as you grow in knowledge, your humility should increase in how you serve the surrounding community with that knowledge, and still how comparatively little you know. Pride is a quick road to being rendered ineffective. And people are usually fairly good at sensing arrogance. So, again, keep your view of yourself in check. We are not ever as smart as we think we are, no matter how many books we have read or what schools we have attended.

At the same time, we should ever desire to be life-long learners. "Let the enlargement of your knowledge," exhorts Watts, "be one constant view and design in life; since there is no time or place, no transaction, occurrences, or engagements in life, which exclude this method of improving the mind." [58] We should delight in and be stimulated by gaining knowledge in all kinds of things; from the creepy-crawlers of the world to the economic intricacies of the United States democracy. We should be interested while not thinking a little knowledge means an expertise. Listen. Be patient. Know when to open your mouth. Know when to close it. Don't be afraid to say, "I don't know." More on this later. For now, the final three sections will lend themselves to increasing both one's conviction of what one *does know* and one's humility in what one *does not know*.

3. Observe. The world is at our fingertips. No, not like we can conquer the world in one grasp, but that we are always, on all sides and at all times of life surrounded by things to learn. Think about it. We are part of a larger story. You are a single character in a story which has been going on for thousands of years through a multitude of generations. You plopped down in history at a particular time within a particular setting. At all times you are somewhere in this story. And at all times our senses are available to know the surrounding stage. Smell. Lick. Listen. See. Tickle. What is this stuff? Who are you? Why is all of this happening?

Observe the natural world. Dig up the things that crawl and move, the kind which makes your sister sing high soprano. Observe the beasts of the field and birds of the air. Pick a continent and start looking at the creepy-crawlies. Observe and experience, as best you can, the vast intricacies of God's design. Listen to others' stories of the natural world. Ask them questions. Gain both direct and indirect experiences of God's designed stage, the stage upon which your life will play out. Experiencing something as alien as the depths of the oceans, heights of mountains, and non-solace of caves will, believe it or not, give you a better storehouse of information from which you can draw metaphors and helpful information for reasonably relating to others. Augustine in his *De Doctrina Christiana* called this being acquainted with 'things' rather than symbols. The laws of logic are alive and well outside the classroom in our most elementary experiences, and these are often embodied in our perception and understanding of the natural world. Likewise, great materials for creating great metaphors for describing and understanding logic are all around us in the natural world. Watts reminds us, "

> When we are in the house or the city, wheresoever we turn our eyes, we see the works of men; when we are abroad in the country, we behold more of the works of God. The skies and the ground above and beneath us, and the animal and vegetable world round about us, may entertain our observation with ten thousand varieties...fetch down knowledge from the clouds, the stars, the sun, the moon, and the revolutions of all the planets. Dig and draw up some valuable meditations from the depths of the earth, and search them through the vast oceans of water.

Extract some intellectual improvements from the minerals and metals; from the wonders of nature among the vegetables and herbs, trees and flowers. Learn some lessons from the birds and the beasts, and the meanest insect. Read the wisdom of God, and his admirable contrivance in them all: read his almighty power, his rich and various goodness, in all the works of his hands." [59]

Similarly, *observe the other characters in the story.* Look around when you are at the grocery store. Observe the conversation which occurs at the orange crate, near the frozen food section. Be comfortable in observing and asking questions of your immediate surroundings. In short, watch the stories in the present. Know your culture and the culture of your opponent. Watch people talk. Listen to people's conversations. Observe the awkwardness. Place yourself within the awkwardness. Crowd the things that are crowding you and peer into the vast reality that is your present reality. Look for patterns. Look for themes. They are there, and recognizing them will aid your ability to use reasonable and pertinent arguments for whatever occasion. And as you observe, ask questions to yourself and even of those around you. Why is *this* Starbucks designed this way? Why use those colors? Why coffee? Why is this man reading the newspaper every time I see him?

There is a story being told, and if you want to enter it in argument form, you need to understand the stage. What is the story of your community? What is the story of your school? Your family? Your friends? Your foes? As a friend once instructed me, "The more you know, the more you can know, and the more your argument will be informed with depth and breadth." Observation matters for all knowledge. There is no situation from which you cannot learn. This is what Watts was encouraging when he said, "From the vicissitudes and revolutions of nations and families, and from the various occurrences of the world, learn the instability of mortal affairs, the uncertainty of life, the certainty of death. From a coffin and a funeral, learn to meditate upon your own departure. From the vices and follies of others, observe what is hateful in them; consider how such a practice looks in another person, and remember that it looks as ill or worse in yourself. From the virtues of others, learn something worthy of your imitation."[60] Similarly, "Endeavor therefore to derive instruction or improvement of the mind from every thing which you see or hear, from every thing which occurs in human life, from every thing within you or without you...Thus from every appearance in nature, and from every occurrence of life, you may derive natural, moral, and religious observations, to entertain your minds, as well as rules of conduct in the affairs relating to this life and that which is to come." [61]

Observing and studying those things which are always around you grants an awareness and familiarity which has long been lost in our own day. Many have called this *common sense*. It could also be called extrabiblical knowledge, knowledge found outside the Christian Scriptures. J.P. Moreland is helpful in briefly explaining this idea. "God has revealed Himself and various truths on a number of topics outside the Bible. As Christians have known throughout our history, common sense, logic, and mathematics – along with the arts, humanities, sciences, and other areas of study – contain important truths relevant to life in general and to the development of a careful, life-related Christian worldview. According to the Bible, wisdom comes from studying ants as well as learning Scripture (Proverbs 6)!" [62]

Thus, you should never say "I'm bored." In doing so you show your lack of observation and ingenuity. You show your deep ingratitude. You live on a sphere of dirt and water which is hurdling through space in a constant pattern. Mathematically, you should not exist in this present moment. Philosophically, it would be impossible for you to exist in any other moment. And covering your body you have a coat of living fabric which heals itself. All you have to do is take a bite of pizza. Never forget the magic behind it all, and take Watts's advice. "Let your hope of new discoveries, as well as the satisfaction and pleasure of known truths, animate your daily industry." [63]

4. Read. Read. Read. Read wide. Read thin. Read deep. Read shallow. If you get a monthly allowance from your parents, emulate Isaac Watts in his younger years when upon receiving a few coins from his mother, he said, "Book. Book. Buy a book!" Don't just read what interests you. Read what interests your friend. Read what interests your enemy. Read old stuff. Read new stuff. Read novels. *Read poetry!* Read magazines. Read articles. Read dictionaries. Read books about cultural clichés. Read books on metaphors. Read books about modern tree-houses. Read essays. Read plays. Regularly review texts on formal and informal logic. Re-read one lesson each week. Re-mind yourself of truths previously learned. Read movie scripts. Read nursery rhymes, and do not think you're ever too old to stop. Read instruction manuals. Try to draw an instruction manual. Read cookbooks. Read aloud. Read silently. *Argument always has content.* There is subject matter to every argument. And you will not be able to speak intelligently or deeply if you do not have a depth and breadth to the content about which you argue. Again, the more you know, the more you can know.

This is a pretty basic concept. You would not be able to argue well for the beauty of Scripture had you never read it. How difficult would it be to argue that Shakespeare is one of the best English poets if you had never even read Shakespeare, or any other English poet? I'm sure you could memorize some argument and just spit it out, but that is not what street-fighting logic is about.

In street-fighting logic, you must think on your toes. You must have a kind of smarts: street smarts. Not to mention, rote argument apart from true understanding and ownership is deceptive; it is the wrong, lying kind. It is like a boxer who choreographs his whole fight, not ever willing or able to improvise when needed. And we all know how that ends up. So, to present good arguments you must have good knowledge. One of the best ways to get this kind of street smarts is by reading. By reading widely, you will get to know the proofs and arguments for many different subject areas (science, Bible, history, literature, arithmetic, culinary arts, *et cetera*). The employment of street-fighting logic is not just about a good use of the logical techniques, but a good use of logic within a subject area. *Remember, content is the difference between a valid argument and a sound argument.*

So, what to read? In short, everything age and biblically appropriate. All that I mentioned at the start of this section (poems, dictionaries, movie scripts, *ad infinitum*) is fair game. Obviously, if you are still under your parents' mediation, run the piece of literature by them. But you get the idea. Go for it. The two main sections here would fall under history and literature, and even the historical works do not cease from being works of literature in the broad sense. Thucydides and Caesar can attest to this.

History is compiled of the stories that God has bothered to tell with mankind. By reading history, a number of great things can happen. First, you can get to know man. Second, you can get to know God. Third, you can get to know the patterns of history, the patterns of God's story told with man. Knowing this story will be central to knowing arguments that have come before you. If you think you are the first Christian to argue for the importance of the incarnation, you are wrong. It has been necessary time and again. Being familiar with the history of God's world will familiarize you with what has been done and how it worked out for those guys and gals. How did the fall of Rome affect Augustine's arguments set forth in *The City of God*? What has been the relationship between Christians and Muslims throughout history? Surely the answers to these questions are important, especially if your argument cross-references any of it. As the Roman historian Livy says in his preface to *The History of Rome*, "This it is which is particularly salutary and profitable in the study of history, that you behold instances of every variety of conduct displayed on a conspicuous monument; that from thence you may select for yourself and for your country that which you may imitate; thence note what is shameful in the undertaking, and shameful in the result, which you may avoid."

Literature is the poetic, prosaic, and imaginative work of the those who have come before us and some who are still among us. Literature is invaluable, and that of the Western tradition holds some of the most radiant gold the world has ever seen. There are numerous reasons for why we should read the authors who wrote it. We call them the *classics*. And if a student is classically educated, he should do his homework. Among the crowd sits Homer, Aeschylus, Plato, Aristotle, Virgil, Augustine, Dante, Chaucer, Shakespeare, Chesterton, Lewis, and many, many more. These will be covered in greater depth in later chapters. But, for now, we must give a basic affirmation to how literature provides a kind of knowledge that is wholly different from other kinds. To do so, we need not look any further than a classic author in his own right, the father of the Italian Renaissance, Petrarch. The following quotes do well to stand alone:

"Neither exhortations to virtue nor the argument of approaching death should divert us from literature; for in a good mind it excites the love of virtue, and dissipates, or at least diminishes, the fear of death. To desert our studies shows want of self-confidence rather than wisdom, for letters do not hinder but aid the properly constituted mind which possesses them; they facilitate our life, they do not retard it. Just as many kinds of food which lie heavy on an enfeebled and nauseated stomach furnish excellent nourishment for one who is well but famishing, so in our healthy intellect, especially if in our use of both food and learning we exercise proper discretion." [64]

"However, let me not pass over in silence the more obvious pleasures: to devote oneself to reading and writing, alternately finding employment and relief in each, to read what our forerunners have written and to write what later generations may wish to read, to pay to posterity the debt which we cannot pay to the dead for the gift of their writings, and yet not remain altogether ungrateful to the dead but to make their names more popular if they are little known, to restore them if they have been forgotten, to dig them out if they have been buried in the ruins of time and to hand them down to our grandchildren as objects of veneration, to carry them in the heart and as something sweet in the mouth, and finally, by cherishing, remembering, and celebrating their fame in every way, to pay them the homage that is due to their genius even though it is not commensurate with their greatness." [65]

"Then there are books of different kinds in whose substance and whose authors one has pleasant, unfailing companions, ready at his bidding to go into public or return to his house, always prepared to be silent or to speak, to stay at home or to accompany him in the woods, to travel, to remain in the country, to converse, to amuse, to cheer, to comfort, to advise, to dispute, to consult, to teach the secrets of nature, the memorable deeds of history, the rule of life and the contempt of death, moderation in prosperity, fortitude in adversity, equanimity and steadfastness in all our actions; cheerful associates, learned, humble, and eloquent, free from annoyance and expense, without complaint or grumbling, without envy or treachery. Add to all these benefits that they do not ask for food or drink and are content with scant raiment and a narrow portion of the house, though they afford their hosts inestimable treasures of mind, spacious houses, brilliant attire, delightful entertainment, and most savory food." [66]

It can hardly be said better. And any meager explanation presented here will detract from what should be consistent re-readings of these three quotes. Read them again. Sure, now. Let them wash over you, cleanse you, like all good literature should. And when choosing literature, the food for your soul, be not afraid that a Christian emblem does not cover the front page. As John Wesley once stated, "To imagine none can teach you but those who are themselves saved from sin, is a very great and dangerous mistake. Give not place to it for a moment." [67] This has been not only a tenable position throughout Christian church history, but a desirable one, a biblical one.

In 1667 the Reformed pastor Richard Baxter wrote a book to meet the lukewarm and unbelieving needs of his time. In it he appealed to philosophy, logic, and extra-biblical knowledge to argue his point. Similarly, Augustine has been a towering figure throughout history, championing this grand idea of extra-biblical knowledge: "We must show our Scriptures not to be in conflict with whatever [our critics] can demonstrate about the nature of things from reliable sources." His personal journey as told in his *Confessions* shows how the literary works of writers such as Plato and Cicero were helpful in his increasing knowledge of and love for the Triune God. And as Watts reminds us,

> "Seize upon truth where'er 'tis found,
> Amongst your friends, amongst your foes,
> On Christian or on Heathen ground;
> The flower's divine sweet where'er it grows,
> Neglect the prickles and assume the rose." [68]

Your time of study should be littered and loaded with good literature. In short, your time of study should aim to be what Richard Foster rightly explains as "...a specific kind of experience in which through careful observation of objective structures we cause thought processes to move in a certain way...When done with concentration, perception and repetition, ingrained habits of thought are formed." [69]

Yet, in all this affirmation of reading, I must here present a warning. We must be strategic in how and what we read. Quantity and quality are not the same things, and "life is too short, and time is too precious, to read every new book quite over in order to find that it is not worth the reading." [70] Take Mortimer Adler's advice from his *How to Read a Book*: when approaching a book you should first skim the table of contents. If it seems worth further study, read the introduction. Still tastes good? Read the first paragraph of each chapter. If each step confirms your high appreciation of what the author has to say, continue further still until you have devoured the whole. Then, continue your judicious appraisal in light of other works of its kind. This will save you both time and energy from being wasted on lesser goods.

Working at Barnes and Noble and devouring all they have to sell to the unsuspecting consumer does not necessarily offer real and true knowledge for life and godliness. Armchair philosophers may beg to differ. But while reading in and of itself is innately good and offers its faithful a host of blessings, it offers little to the undiscerning human, the street-fighting logician not aimed toward that active life of virtue, wisdom, and faith. As Watts says of this topic, "A well-furnished library, and a capacious memory, are indeed of singular use toward the improvement of the mind; but if all your learning be nothing else but a mere amassment of what others have written, without a due penetration into the meaning, and without a judicious choice and determination of your own sentiments, I do not see what title your head has to true learning above your shelves." As Christians, we do not want to be walking bookshelves. Likewise, street-fighting logic is the kind of discipline which is often more concerned with quality than quantity. Wit is the kind of thing which is deeply discerning, and as will be explained later, wit is one of the most important components of real-time, intellectual grappling. Thus, "In all our studies and pursuits of knowledge, let us remember that virtue and vice, sin and holiness, and the conformation of our hearts and lives to the duties of true religion and morality, are things of far more consequent than all the furnishings of our understanding, and the richest treasures of more speculative knowledge..."[71] And in another place, "As you are not to fancy yourself a learned man because you are blessed with a ready wit: so neither must you imagine that a large and laborious reading, and a strong memory, can denominate you truly wise." [72]

Even further, taking all our students learn in their yeas of logic and applying it to their time of reading is just as important as applying it to their time of conversation. It is often in times of isolated quiet that some of us are most vulnerable to believe and convince ourselves of almost anything. As Watts states of this sentiment, "Books are never to be judged of merely by their subject, or the opinion they represent, but by the justness of their sentiment, the beauty of their manner, the force of their expression, or the strength of reason, and the weight of just and proper argument which appears in them." [73] Reiterating what was said earlier, street-fighting logic is the kind of thing which does not seem to go away. It always occurs, and thus we must be ready in season and out of season to account for what we hold to be true.

Finally on this subject of books and the warning thereof, I will allow more of Watts's words to run their course over our hearts and minds.

> "I confess those whose reading is designed only to fit them for much talk and little knowledge, may content themselves to run over their authors in such a sudden and trifling way; they may devour libraries in this manner, yet be poor reasoners at least; and have no solid wisdom or true learning. The traveller who walks on fair and softly in a course that points right, and examines every turning before he ventures upon it, will come sooner and safer to his journey's end, than he who runs through every lane he meets, though he gallops full speed all day. The man of much reading, and a large retentive memory, but without meditation, may become in the sense of the world a knowing man; and if he converse much with the ancients, he may attain the name of learning too; but he spends his days afar off from wisdom and true judgment, and possesses very little of the substantial riches of the mind." [74]

5. *Recognize.* We must know our limitations. And we, each one of us, will always have limitations. Thus, you would do well to know

your own ignorance. Not only should we know when to open our mouth, we should know when to close it. Very few things are more repulsive than the student who thinks a few good grades in a few hard classes gives him grounds to know anything about everything. This is not the spirit of Christianity. It is not honest. It is deceptive, and usually so because of great arrogance and pride. Petrarch once said, "For can there be a wider field, a vaster ground for talking, than a treatise on ignorance and especially on mine?" [75] This posture should likewise be ours. Watts instructs, "You should therefore contrive and practice some proper methods to acquaint yourself with your own ignorance, and to impress your mind with a deep and painful sense of the low and imperfect degrees of your present knowledge, that you may be incited with labour and activity to pursue after greater measures." [76] A deeper knowledge of one's ignorance should promote study, interest, and appreciation.

The great Reformer John Calvin in his *Institutes of the Christian Religion* echoes a similar posture toward our own knowledge, or the lack thereof. "But knowledge of ourselves lies first in considering what we were given at creation and how generously God continues his favor toward us, in order to know how great our natural excellence would be if only it had remained unblemished; yet at the same time to bear in mind that there is in us nothing of our own, but that we hold on sufferance whatever God has bestowed upon us. Hence we are ever depended on him. Secondly, to call to mind our miserable condition after Adam's fall; the awareness of which, when all our boasting and self-assurance are laid low, should truly humble us and overwhelm us with shame." [77] A deeper knowledge of one's ignorance should promote humility and gratitude.

According to Nicholas of Cusa, there is a kind of learned ignorance which occurs with greater and greater learning. Yes, as you learn more, you are able to learn more. But as you learn more, you are more capable of seeing how much more you do not know. It is like ascending an eternal mountain. Are you actually ascending? Yes. Does your view with every step allow you to look down and see all you have hiked? Yes. Simultaneously, every step will reveal the depth and grandeur you have yet to ascend, not only on this mountain but on every surrounding one. Watts correctly explains this tension between a love of learning and an appraisal of one's ignorance. "No man is obliged to learn and know every thing; this can neither be sought nor required, for it is utterly impossible: yet all persons are under some obligation to improve their own understanding; otherwise it will be a barren desert, or a forest overgrown with weeds and brambles. Universal ignorance or infinite errors will overspread the mind, which is utterly neglected, and lies without any cultivation." [78] I have often said that one who receives his Master's degree has only mastered the ability to confidently say he is a master of no thing. Similarly, a Ph.D. primarily grants to its recipient the clarifying ability to diagnose the depths of his own ignorance. Again, hear and consider Watts's words. "Remember this, that if upon some few superficial acquirements you value, exalt, and swell yourself, as though you were a man of learning already, you are thereby building a most unpassable barrier against all improvement; you will lie down and indulge idleness, and rest yourself contended in the midst of deep and shameful ignorance." [79] Just as a deeper knowledge of one's ignorance should promote study, interest, appreciation, humility, and gratitude, so it should promote hard work, a life of labor.

In the end, a humble man is one who can recognize and confess with joyful confidence, not shame, his own ignorance. This is a man who truly knows what it means to be man. This is a defining mark of the man of letters, the man who hungers for truth yet never presumes himself full. Ultimately, when speaking of our learning and ignorance, let us be able to say with Petrarch, "I am not so fortunate in what I achieve as passionate in my work, being much more of a lover of learning than a man who has got much of it." [80]

The affirmation of one's ignorance, contrary to what our modern beliefs about self-esteem may say, lead not to total depression and suppression of love and desire, or an abiding lack of enthusiasm to grow in learning. If done properly, a right appraisal of one's ignorance should lead to a joyful climb upward, not a downtrodden fall into shame and self-hatred. What comes from confessing one's ignorance is not a curse, but a blessing. "As you should carry about with you a constant and sincere sense of your own ignorance," Watts states, "so you should not be afraid nor ashamed to confess this ignorance, by taking all proper opportunities to ask and inquire for farther information; whether it be the meaning of a word, the nature of a thing, the reason of a proposition, the custom of a nation, &c. never remain in ignorance for want of asking...God and man are ready to teach the meek, the humble, and the ignorant; but he that fancies himself to know any particular subject well, or that will not venture to ask a question about it, such a one will not put himself into the way of improvement by inquiry and diligence." [81]

For the street-fighting logician, training is an everyday grind. It is a 'plod and moil' mentality. It is one which can truly make you a renaissance man, in *many* senses of that word. And if you have not picked it up yet, it must be explicitly stated that the street-fighting logician is no intellectual elitist. He is no devout specialist or high talker. He must be an everyday man, a man of common life and common language. He must not think anything too beneath his acquaintance with, his practice in, and his employment of knowledge. He should gain just as much from the town drunk as he does from the town scholar. His inquiry and interest in those in the nursing home should not be overshadowed by his interest in those of the university. Between constant observation, civic involvement, and quiet retreats to a place of study, the trained life of the one who rightly employs street-fighting logic revels in a tension between the active and contemplative life. And this tension is humbling. Living and maturing in this tension yields the kinds of rewards that permeate all areas of life (spiritual, physical, emotional, *et cetera*). This training will not just change one's grade point average but is meant to alter one's relationship with parents, siblings, teachers, and the random train car stranger. It is the kind of training that is worldview shaping. It makes you a different kind of person, rather than just a different kind of student. In short, this training is driven by love, the real kind.

So, what of this training? What are the results? This training seeks to prevent the too-often-affirmed 'kaleidoscope Christianity', the spliced and unfocused vision of God and his truth, as well as the 'sound-byte Christianity', those who know bits of incoherent and unrelated biblical facts. The training encouraged here should grant to its gainful employer a 'symphonic Christianity', a full and robust view of the things of man and the things of God in light of truth, where'er 'tis found. It is to be virtuous. Redemptive. If our intellectual inquiries are not somehow tied to truths that lead back to God, then our indulgence in them is likely a form of forgetfulness, of idolatry. It is simply acquiring a cast of mind which fritters away intellectual energies. It is a kind of hiding God from yourself. We should oppose that which Augustine opposed: the defining and conditioning of the intellect to lose itself in the superficial, and not inquire into how it leads back to God. In this way, we must in our training see God's grace and providence rightly, how it rightly transcends more than Christian bookstores.

Though James Nance is specifically discussing the rules of inference, I believe his words in lesson fifteen of *Intermediate Logic* ring true for all aspects of logic. They are especially true for our training in street-fighting logic and for the artistry therein. "Read over them a few times. They are the tools of the art, and a good artist is familiar with all his paints and his brushes because he constantly uses them, trying new things with them, mixing them in different ways, and so on. A good artist practices…remember that you are exercising your mind…your brain is maturing and growing like your muscles mature and grow. Give it time." [82]

Finally, in your training, play. Pray. Know. Observe. Read. Recognize. And be not afraid to dig. Ask questions. Leave no rock unturned, for while you live you have the privilege of experiencing the kind of life angels envy. So, hear Francis Schaeffer's words. "The ancients were afraid that if they went to the end of the earth they would fall off and be consumed by dragons. But once we understand that Christianity is true to what is there, true to the ultimate environment – the infinite, personal God who is really there – then our minds are freed. We can pursue any question and can be sure that we will not fall off the end of the earth." [83]

Focus Questions.

1. What five exercises matter most for the street-fighting logician's training?
2. How can training take place in one's everyday life?
3. What is the difference between a sound argument and a valid argument?
4. Why does prayer matter for the one who wants a strong mind?
5. What does it take to be an observant person?
6. Recognition is a part of logic, but what should a person recognize to become a good logician?
7. What is the importance of reading good literature?
8. What is one of the prominent marks of a humble person?
9. How can you practice these five disciplines every day?

Exercises.

1. Ask a complete stranger if they took a class on logic, and then ask them what it would take for someone to be a good debater. Record their answer and be ready to discuss.
2. Look around your home. Find a common object from everyday life and write a 150-200 word essay on what you can learn from it. How might that object find its way into a debate?
3. Go to a local grave yard and make twenty new observations you have not made before. Your observations should cover all the senses.

4.   Imagine you are at a local restaurant. Two people are at the table next to you discussing your favorite subject. Not only do they hold a view contrary to yours, but they are loud and obnoxious about their positon, laughing and carrying on. They see you look over a few times, so they ask if you have any thoughts on the subject. You want to make a worthwhile contribution. In no less than 250 words, explain how the five disciplines in this chapter would apply particularly to this situation.

Chapter 3
The Strategy

"I was not interested in learning what he [Ambrose] was talking about. My ears were only for his rhetorical technique; this empty concern was all that remained with me after I had lost any hope that a way to you [God] might lie open for man. Nevertheless together with the words which I was enjoying, the subject matter, in which I was unconcerned, came to make an entry into my mind. I could not separate them. While I opened my heart in noticing the eloquence with which he spoke, there also entered no less the truth which he affirmed, though only gradually." Augustine[84]

"A person may have a strong reason and yet not have a good reason. He may have a strength of mind to drive an argument, yet not hold even balances. It is not so much from a defect of the reasoning process, as from a fault of the disposition – if by the dictate of the understanding is meant what reason declares to be best or most for the person's happiness taken in the whole of his duration, it is not true that the will always follows the last dictate of the understanding." Jonathan Edwards[85]

"As Christians we must of course repent of all the anger, malice, and self-will which allowed the discussion to become, on our side, a quarrel at all." C.S. Lewis[86]

"If there are no values higher than biological ones, it is necessary to call man a 'diseased animal' with and in spite of his civilization. And as a consequence, man's thinking, too, becomes a form of his disease." Max Scheler[87]

"Good logic is an instrument of persuasion; it is only one ingredient in a larger interpersonal situation; and those who love logic and are good at it often forget the context. Intelligent people's minds are not changed by bad logic, but they are not changed by bad personal tactics either." Peter Kreeft[88]

Once an adequate amount of training has occurred, how should one go about practicing street-fighting logic? Which strategies are appropriate and which strategies are counterproductive? Strategy is the kind of thing that allows underdogs to take down behemoths. It is also the kind of thing that allows behemoths to surrender willingly, sacrificially, to underdogs. It is plan. It is execution. It is diplomacy, discretion, judgment, skill, delicacy, perception, dexterity, and insight. It is moment by moment decision making in the heat of the battle. Without strategy, street-fighting logic becomes a guessing game; a kind of blind-man-playing-billiards scenario. Thus, we must make every strike strategic. And if we tap out, we must do so for more than reasons of self-preservation. This is no *Hunger Games* arena. It is life. And usually strategy means saving others before you attempt to save yourself.

It was once said, by either Howard W. Newton or Isaac Newton (no one is really sure anymore) that tact is the art of making a point without making an enemy. The problem with this definition of tact is that for any person who seeks to promote and live according to the truth, enemies are inevitable. Some men are so prone to cynicism and living contrary that they will necessarily make themselves enemies of anything. Thus, the better portrait of tact would be, "Tact is the art of making a point while making the right kinds of enemies." The presence of enemies does not make someone tactless. Likewise, the absence of enemies does not make someone tactful.

The broader canvas we must set before applying distinct colors regarding the street-fighting logician's strategy is that our lives, and all things of life, are deeply personal. In Christian doctrine, truth does not take place in a vacuum or abstract realm, but within a world which is inhabited and created by persons. The quest for truth is a personal quest. This does not mean that any statement whatsoever can be true as long as one person claims it as such, or that any person can determine his or her own truth. It simply means that the incarnation of Christ, and the claims which Christ made that he is the way, the *truth*, and the life should have a significant effect upon how we as Christians understand truth claims. Again, this is not to say that some propositions are not universally true, or that a syllogism which does not mention the divinity of Christ is somehow unsound. It is to say that truth is always related to a person, and truth-values are always determined by personal beings.

The basis for logic, the three laws of thought, are true because they relate to an ultimate authority, a personal being which exists above and beyond those truth claims. Simply put, laws cannot exist or be upheld outside of a law-giver. In the same way, truth cannot exist apart from at least one person who ultimately has knowledge of all truth, who can determine whether this one truth is consistent with all possible truths. And, as Christians, we believe an omniscient God fits that requirement quite nicely. Not only do we believe that an omniscient God fulfills that requirement, but we likewise believe that this same omniscient God can impart truth into his creatures, placing us in a world which allows for discovering truth. This discovery means we may know something truly even though we may not know it perfectly or fully. With that said, let us next consider why one's rhetoric requires that one account for the personhood of the listener.

Presentation matters, which means the way a truth is presented (rhetoric) and the truth which is presented (logic) should not be thought of as mutually exclusive disciplines. Rhetoric, like logic, is personal. All argumentation is. Anything ever dealing with words is personal. Street-fighting logic deals with the person speaking and the person listening. For Cicero, one of the greatest of the ancient rhetoricians, eloquence and truth could not be divided. You may know truth by the way it is presented, with an eloquence of speech. Or one who is attune to good rhetoric may disregard a truth because of its seemingly vulgar presentation. This is one reason why Augustine, when turning to Scripture, threw it aside. He found a lower language than he expected, and therefore assumed it was void of truth. This is another reason why he returned to the Scriptures and came to love them, once he met Bishop Ambrose, who, with eloquence taught Scripture to Augustine and opened Scripture's rhetoric beauty to him.

In the art of street-fighting logic, our strategy must account for the personhood of *this* person, the one with whom we speak. Our demeanor, response, and suggestions must account for the 'personness' of our opponent. It must also account for the 'personness' of one's self. We should be aware of how persons dialogue differently than machines or brute beasts, how they interact and best receive information. We must be aware of the difference between communication and communion, as the Southern literary critic Allen Tate so wonderfully expressed. And in our day in age, we must realize that talking to someone in person is different than communicating to a screen, as I am doing in typing these words. When it comes to strategy, there are ten characteristics your conversation should carry. And you should seek to consciously carry these to fruition throughout your interaction with your opponent.

1. Listen. The art of listening well is just as important in the war of words as is the art of speaking well. As a kind of observing, listening well is the first and arguably most important strategy to be mastered. Even still, though listening is the first form of communication we learn as humans, listening is an all too often neglected art. As Adler states in *How to Speak How to Listen*, "How extraordinary is the fact that no effort is made anywhere in the whole educational process to help individuals learn how to listen well – at least well enough to close the circuit and make speech effective as a means of communication…however low the level of writing and reading is today among those who have the advantages of twelve or more years of schooling, much lower still is the level of skill in speaking that most people possess, and lowest of all is skill in listening." [89] A good listener, the effective and active listener who is truly anticipating patterns, nuances, particulars, and universals, has more than likely gained a better understanding of his opponent than his opponent has of his own position. We too often are a people who don't listen well, even to ourselves. It can therefore be surprising when others do it so well, to the point where they recognize something about us which we have yet to notice. It is striking. It is attractive, like when someone remembers your name after the first time meeting them. There begins an automatic relationship and acknowledgement of persons.

Another important component to listening well is not only its potential to place you on higher ground strategically in the debate, but it also shows a genuine care for your opponent and their thoughts. And as a friend once told me, people do not care how much you know until they know how much you care. You can never underestimate the power of a listening ear. You may just find that it can disarm an opponent faster than a sound syllogism. And if not, you are being faithful to love your neighbor well, in respecting their conclusions as real conclusions whether or not they are ugly monsters of heresy. Even if you don't gain a like-minded brother after the debate, listening well will at least gain you a friend.

Do not listen well for the sake of your reputation. Listen well like a good doctor listens well, so that whatever illness may exist in your opponent, you may more readily cure it with the proper remedy, as you would want them to do for you. As Watts stated, "...hear the argument with patience, though it differ ever so much from your sentiments, for you yourself are very desirous to be heard with patience by others who differ from you. Let not your thought be active and busy all the while to find out something to contradict, and by what means to oppose the speaker, especially in matters which are not brought to an issue. This is a frequent and unhappy temper and practice. You should rather be intent and solicitous to take up the mind and meaning of the speaker, zealous to seize and approve all that is true in his discourse, nor yet should you want courage to oppose where it is necessary; but let your modesty and patience, and a friendly temper, be as conspicuous as your zeal." [90]

So, what kind of things can a good listener expect to hear in a dispute? First, you should expect to hear the kinds of things you know exist. If you do not know how to spot an informal fallacy, you will not recognize one in word or deed. So, keep training. Upon training well, listen for certain terms. What terms are being used? How is that term being defined? Have there been any contradictions of terms? Likewise, be on the lookout for authorities. No, not cops. Listen for who your opponent sights as an authority on a subject. What academic discipline do they tend to site as having authority? What kind of metaphors are being used which might expose whether they see philosophy or literature as a higher authority for human knowledge? Where do they argue circularly, back to ultimate authorities? Are they their own authority on the subject? What does that tell you?

Again, be on the lookout for fallacies. Those who have studied *Introductory Logic* should listen for the glaring presence of one of the informal fallacies. So, as was encouraged in the last chapter, review those on a regular basis. And sharpen your ability to clearly see them in everyday circumstances, outside of the classroom. As Adler states, "Understanding what the speaker is trying to say, perceiving how he or she is managing to say it, and noting the reasons or the arguments advanced for the conclusions that the speaker seeks to have adopted are indispensable to effective listening, just as they are dispensable to effective reading." [91]

Simultaneously, look for what is below the speaker's words. This most certainly includes reading body language. When speaking of signs by which we communicate, Augustine said, "Some of the signs by which people communicate their feelings to one another concern the eyes; most of them concern the ears, and a very small number concern the other senses...All these things are, to coin a phrase, visible words." [92] This often takes ingenuity and careful induction and deduction so as to not misrepresent the speaker, even in your own mind. But listen for intent just as much as for content. This is a kind of listening which may involve more than your ears. Just as well, listen for your own intent. Intent comes before content. Another way of saying this is you must envision before you inscribe. With envisioning, you see relationships as they are and foresee relationships as you think they ought to be. This goes for both the one who speaks knowledge and the crotchety professor who simply wants to throw a college freshman off their religious high horse. With inscribing, we begin to move the world, and the beings therein, into a relationship we think suitable to their cause. Speaking, like all acts of creation and sub-creation, is preceded by the intentions of the speaker. By being aware of a speaker's intentions, as best as we can, we may more readily discern the broader worldview of the speaker, his conclusions on a subject, and his intent and sentiment for remaining in the present conversation. In short, listening helps you discern your opponent's need of the hour, which will in turn enable you to give a proper, real-time diagnosis of why the disagreement exists and what kind of disagreement it proves to be. Proverbs says it this way: "If one gives an answer before he hears, it is his folly and shame." (Prov. 18:13)

2. *Ask.* When Socrates and Jesus agree on something, we would do well to listen. Both Socrates and Jesus knew the importance of asking questions. Questions are one of the most non-combative ways to dialogue with someone. Ironically, they can also be the most combative way to dialogue with someone. Socrates was notorious for this. His unique approach to testing other's wisdom as he went throughout Athens eventually led to his death. If Athens was a horse, he likened himself to a gadfly. The apathy of our current culture, and the propensity to lead lives which are thoroughly inconsistent with one's worldview, or what one professes to be their ethical and religious beliefs, calls for us to act a bit like Socrates. We should probe. We should investigate. We should hope that our love for truth, and for the integrity of that truth in our society, would create in us a discontent for the unhealthy aspects of our contemporary culture. Likewise, Jesus used questions for a number of reasons, one being so that he could expose for either his opponent or for a nearby listener the glaring problems in his opponent's thoughts, words, or deeds.

If used well, the Socratic method has a natural ability to disarm and engage your opponent. It puts the 'ball in their court,' and causes them to think for themselves, often coming to conclusions on their own. Preaching and monologues have their place, and this place is a good one, but they do not need to leave that place without a wise and mature handling. Depending on the context, some ways of conveying an idea are better than others. In street-fighting logic, questions are the best strategy for creating an ongoing dialogue without building unnecessary walls between you and your opponent.

As I mentioned, questions are a good way of helping opponents come to their own conclusions. The mind's eye is such that it will trust its own experiences before trusting someone else's. That is to say, one's own ability to 'see the light' is more arresting than hearing someone else's story of seeing that same light. Also, your ability to ask questions is closely related with your ability to listen. If you listen well to a glaring inconsistency, you should be able to ask a relevant question about that inconsistency. If you listen well to a glaring consistency, you should want to learn more about that glaring consistency and if it proves any of your held beliefs true or false. Consequently, you can ask questions to a friend just as easily as you could a foe. In listening well, we should take Adler's advice and ask ourselves four questions during any speech or debate: What is the whole speech about? What are the main or pivotal ideas? Are the speaker's conclusions sound or mistaken? What of it? These questions, when applied to informal conversations or street-fighting debates on a given topic, would more appropriately be stated a bit differently: What is this conversation about? What are the main or pivotal ideas in this conversation? Are my opponent's conclusions sound or mistaken? What of it?

Genuine questions also show a care for the person. They show that you are curious to further discover who your opponent is and how they got to this place—whether 'place' is a religious stance or ethical stance or anywhere in between and outside. Questions convey interest. So, before positing anything of your own beliefs, seek to understand as reasonably as possible those of your opponent. My students should have picked up by now that I have sometimes gone entire class periods simply asking questions: What do you mean? How did you get to that conclusion? How is that similar to the last chapter? Do you agree? What textual evidence do you have to support your claim? How do you think that relates to the previous story? Do you see a problem in what your classmate just said? Who agrees with their classmate? Who would put their grade on their classmate's answer? Who would bet their hair on their classmate's answer? The girls particularly cringe at the last question.

It is telling that God's first recorded words after the fall of Adam and Eve were in the form of questions. "Where are you?" (Gen. 3:9) "Who told you that you were naked? Have you eaten of the tree of which I commanded you not to eat?" (Gen. 3:11) "What is this that you have done?" (Gen. 3:13) Needless to say, God knew the answer to each of these questions; he still saw fit to question his creation before enacting his sentence upon them.

3. Retain. As your opponent answers questions, do your best to retain the main points, and retain any direction you considered as they were speaking, so that when it is your time to speak you will have something worthwhile to say. Hold tightly to their conclusions, and how they arrived there. Then, if their conclusions are more than one, attempt to synthesize their existence and test their ability to uphold a proper understanding of both God and man. Do this even if you have to write some quick notes on a napkin. No one likes a blank stare, an apparent listener, followed by an irrelevant thought or out-of-left-field response. Very few things will kill one's credibility faster, especially if such non-listening occurs in the context of romance.

Because most street-fighting logic scenarios tend to pop up with little warning, we will likely not have a manuscript of the speaker's words. And their words will probably not be in standard categorical form, nicely laid out for us to chop and dissect. They may be speaking with heightened emotions and within a context which does not easily lend itself to long periods of contemplation between responses. Both parties will likely be speaking in plain language, and could even misuse that language in ways that could confuse the talking points. Again, this is why listening well is so important. You cannot retain what you do not hear. So, be prepared to read between the words being spoken, to a conclusion that the speaker may not explicitly say. Retain those conclusions and sift through your storehouse of wisdom and knowledge for a reply that is fitting for where the conversation is and where the conversation is going. In doing this, continue to recall and retain the main points of the conversation and the big picture of the discussion, which often get lost as the attention focuses on one instance of a larger problem. Ultimately, in retaining, retain the purpose of the overall conversation and the structure of your opponent's position.

4. Be fair. Find common ground and relinquish honest appraisals, even if that means you must do a little searching into your own heart or allegiances. Likewise, avoid the straw-man fallacy by misrepresenting an opponent, whether or not they are present at the debate. As Joel McDurmon states, "One of the most pressing concerns for scholars, students, debaters, and everyone actually, involves the question of representing the truth. By this I mean both how we present our own arguments to the public, and how we represent the arguments of those we disagree with. Representation plays a vital role in the Christian faith, and we must make every effort to treat God and others fairly in what we speak and write." [93] This applies to large issues as well as small. Do you represent what you know to be your brother's true sentiment, even if he were not there? Do you do so even if it places you in a worse light?

In fact, go beyond fairness. Attempt to present your opponent's position better than they can, especially if the conversation is posthumous and therefore your opponent is unable to defend themselves at all. Present their position in a fuller light, with as much clarity, beauty, and integrity as it can hold. If there be a slight benefit of doubt, give it to them. This is both strategic and charitable. It is strategic in as much as their fall will meet with greater acceptance given that you, as well as they, know their true position was weaker than the one defeated. It is charitable because you account for the possibility that they may be misrepresenting their position, or you may be misinterpreting it.

If your opponent says something truthful, be not quick to shoot it down because it did not come from your mouth. Rather, be quick to affirm him for it. This holds whether your opponent is a Christian or non-Christian. Simply because Christians are loved by the Truth and seek to love the Truth, does not mean we are the only ones who may notice truth or appreciate truth. Natural man, by the gift of God's common grace, can find truth, affirm that truth, and live by that truth. And though his soul be not redeemed, the truth he holds is actually true. You will win friends sooner with this strategy than with showing the array of your brilliance. By doing this, you will show the true light of friendship and stray far away from the true darkness of self-exaltation. As Watts so finely put it, "When you come to a dispute in order to find out truth, do not presume that you are certainly possessed of it before-hand. Enter the debate with a sincere design of yielding to reason, on which side soever it appears...take a generous pleasure to espy the first rising beams of truth, though it be on the side of your opponent..." [94]

Simultaneously, be more fit and prone to recognize error in your ways than in your opponent's. This does not mean you may not diligently seek out errors in your opponent. It simply means that clearing out logs from eyes should first apply to you, before you apply it to the splinter so clearly jammed in your opponent's. "Be not so ready," begins Watts, "to charge ignorance, prejudice, and mistake upon others, as you are to suspect yourself of it: and in order to shew how free you are from prejudices, learn to bear contradiction with patience: let it be easy to you to hear your own opinion strongly opposed, especially in matters which are doubtful and disputable, amongst men of sobriety and virtue. Give a patient hearing to arguments on all sides..." [95] Contemporary Christians have a brash and mindless tendency to side with the first person who wears a cross necklace, presuming they are like-minded on all things. I find myself less and less astonished each time I disagree with a Christian brother and agree with a pagan classicist on, let's say, education. Be judicious in your appraisal of arguments, even if the conclusion is one which you would strongly uphold, or the person presenting it is 'on your side'. We would do well to eat with our critics and criticize our comrades. Dance with our foes and dispute our friends. In the end, let no one have grounds to say we neither loved our enemies nor strengthened our allies, for to do both is the most humbling of human affairs. In terms of a specific game plan on setting the most level and clearest playing field, Watts exhorts, "There are some few general rules which should be observed in all debates whatsoever, if we would find out a truth by them, or convince a friend of his error, even though they be not managed according to any settled forms of disputation..." [96]

First, "When persons begin a debate, they should always take care that they are agreed in some general principles or propositions, which either more nearly or remotely affect the question in hand..." [97] Let these common propositions lay a foundation for the mutual hope of conviction. Thus, as might be counter intuitive to many of my student's current practices, given how I hear many of them arguing in the hallway, the argument should begin by searching out as far as one agrees with their opponent. Consider those propositions you both hold true. Consider those principles you both affirm. Set those as a working foundation upon which to construct the frame of the conversation. By doing this, you set both of your feet on a charitable and common surface from which a clearer structure may arise.

Second, "The question should be cleared from all doubtful terms and needless additions; and all things that belong to the question should be expressed in plain and intelligible language." [98] Set the central question out front, in plain language. Strip down as many technical terms as possible and replace them with fervent and lively language which will more brilliantly reflect the worthiness of the topic at hand. Turn the question into an issue, which can either be affirmed or denied. If the debate is on the question "Why do we have to wear these dumb uniforms?" Reframe it as "Whether students at our school should be required to wear uniforms." Declare which words are most appropriate. Should 'should' be replaced with 'could'? Is 'required' the best word for the truth we seek? Seek to determine the sense and meaning of the words in the original thesis, then determine whether these words do justice to the debated concept at hand. This is why philosophers can oftentimes be the worst street-fighting logicians. As Sir Philip Sidney stated in his *The Defense of Poesy*, "For the philosopher, setting down with thorny arguments the bare rules, is so hard of utterance, and so misty to be conceived, that one that hath no other guide but him shall wade in him till he be old before he shall find sufficient cause to be honest. For his knowledge standeth so upon the abstract and general, that happy is that man who may understand him, and more happy that can apply what he doth understand." [99]

Third, "...the precise point of inquiry should be distinctly fixed..." [100] As Watts goes on to say, "...the question in debate should be limited precisely to its special extent, or declared to be taken in its more general sense. As for instance, if two men are contending whether civil government be of divine right or not; here it must be observed, the question is not whether monarchy in one man, or a republic in multitudes of the people, or an aristocracy in a few of the chief, is appointed of God as necessary; but whether the civil government in its most general sense, or in any form whatsoever, is derived from the will and appointment of God. Again, the point of inquiry should be limited further. Thus the question is, not whether government comes from the will of God by the light of divine revelation, for that is granted; but whether it is derived from the will of God by the light of reason too. This sort of specification or limitation of the question, hinders and prevents the disputants from wandering away from the precise point of inquiry." [101] Another way of fixing the precise point of inquiry is to define it by its negative. Take G.K. Chesterton's advice. Chesterton stated the same idea a bit differently. "Any one setting out to dispute anything ought always begin by saying what he does not dispute. Beyond stating what he proposes to prove he should always state what he does not propose to prove." [102]

Fairness in argumentation of all kinds means allowing your opponent as much of the same look at the playing field as you have. Though they may be looking for something quite different, and may even see something quite different, the posture you are to hold is one of clarity and even-handedness, even if your opponent lacks much of both. A fair and charitable street-fighting logician is more likely to win the man, if not both the man and the argument.

5. *Relax.* A fervency of spirit is good. An intensity of love is also good. But an anxiety that you are the last hope for this person in dealing with this topic is simply self-centered. You probably think too highly of your own understanding. In any kind of dispute, we must be able to look beyond the immediate circumstances, which means we must not allow the heat of the moment or the enthusiasm of our emotions to dictate the reality that there is still much life to live, and that this episode in our opponent's life, and ours, is part of a bigger story, one governed by a sovereign Author.

Though it may feel this way in the moment, especially if pride is involved, the present argument will more than likely not be the turning point of a generation. An easy trap to fall into is thinking that if some magnificent change does not happen in your opponent by the end of the conversation, you have failed. This happens in topics of both the religious and mundane. This posture is simply not healthy, and it is not most beneficial to having a genuine argument whatsoever. Don't try to 'seal the deal', unless the immediate context calls for a final conclusion, a complete verdict on the topic at hand. Most impromptu debates are more about planting seeds and watering plants than they are about planting, watering, flowering, and harvesting. Keep in mind that this is one conversation in this person's life. C.S Lewis in his *Reflection on the Psalms* explained this phenomenon. "The very man who has argued you down will sometimes be found, years later, to have been influenced by what you said." [103] Be gentle enough to let them leave and loving enough to give them one takeaway, preferable posed in the form of a question. The lack of conviction they have about your stance by the end of the conversation should not dictate yours. There are three main reasons why relaxing is beneficial for all involved in an argument.

First, relax, because the outcome is ultimately out of your hands. As John Calvin instructs, "...the sun rises upon the earth when God's Word shines upon men; but they do not have its benefit until he who is called the 'Father of Lights' (James 1:17) either gives eyes or opens them. For wherever the Spirit does not cast his light, all is darkness." [104] If you train well and your prayers are centered where they belong, they should lead you to a place of peace and calm about a debate, that the turning of hearts does not belong to you. Yours is the speaking of truth, the planting and watering. The harvest belongs to the Lord. This goes for any topic whatsoever. Thirsty men do not need fire hydrants. They need cups of water, and depending on their maturity on the subject, they might need teacups of water. It is not up to you whether the pure water you offer is properly digested. As Augustine prays to God in his *Confessions*, "...none other than you is the teacher of the truth, wherever and from whatever source it is manifest." [105] If it is out of your hands, it means you cannot and should not strive to be a micro-manager of the argument and its context.

The problem with micro-managers is that they don't understand the nature of their own limitations, or the limitations of their peers. They attempt to meet every problem, even the most minor, head on. Their default is to deal with each problem, not on its own terms, but as if each problem was the same as the last. Micro-managers do not understand that some problems just need to be ignored. Some need to be delegated. Some need to be met head on. And others, usually more than we grant, need to be met with a soft backside followed by a jolly chortle. When we boil it down, micro-managers, especially micro-managers of conversations and arguments, lack the ability to balance, to see the world and its problems in light of a larger narrative, one which has both serious priorities and banal blunders.

Argument is often not so much about one party clearly convincing the other, but a kind of listening by one of the constituents which leads to an increased plausibility, or a possibility, of the conclusions. In other words, the goal of argumentation may not be full persuasion, but a higher likelihood of future persuasion, with or without you present.

Second, relax, because you can see more clearly that way. Though J.P. Moreland is speaking of evangelism proper, his words ring true for all kinds of topics, not just Christianity. "Many times we want to communicate the gospel to friends, coworkers, or relatives. But this can create tension and a certain unnaturalness when we are with them, because we feel pressured to find some seam in the conversation from which we can artificially redirect the discussion to our testimony or something of the sort. If a person has a secular/sacred dichotomy in his life due to a lack of a careful thought-out, integrated Christian worldview, then the gospel will have to be forced into an otherwise secular discussion. But if a person has developed a Christian mind, she can relax because she has an understanding of and a Christian view about a number of 'secular' topics. In such a situation, it would be hard to have a normal conversation without Christianity coming up naturally and in a way relevant to the topic of discussion. Moreover, a well-developed mind can see connections between what a friend is saying and other issues of which the friend may not be aware. For example, a friend may be espousing moral relativism yet inconsistently hold that we still have an absolute duty to save the environment. If a person sees the connections, she can simply ask well-placed questions that naturally lead to a discussion of broader worldview issues, including God and our relationship to Him. In such a case, the pressure is off because a person has the intellectual categories necessary to make natural connections between Christianity and a host of regular conversation topics. There is no need to try to find a crack in the discussion to insert a gospel presentation unrelated to the flow of the conversation. What a joyful fruit of the intellectual life this is!" [106] Now you should more clearly see why training is so important: so that you are more than a one-dimensional person in conversation and disputation. Whether you are speaking of the existence of God or the supremacy of one book over another, you can relax and allow the debate to take its organic shape, which is most fitting given that debates are among persons and not robots. Therefore, relaxation is often the first step to good art, to allowing the imagination to run its course, to allow the Holy Spirit to work His power.

Third, relax, because a peaceful and gentle spirit, though passionate and fervent nonetheless, is agreeable to all men. "Be not fond of disputing every thing pro and con," Watts says, "nor indulge yourself to shew your talent of attacking and defending. A logic which teaches nothing else is little worth." [107] Friendship is not forged in a room of clinched fists, and disputes do not go well when disputants are prone to show their talent of attacking and defending. Narcissism does not bode well for life in community. Just because you have a gun on your belt does not mean your hand should always be on it. A proper employment of logic and argumentation is one tool among many for changing the world and convincing men of the truth. More on this later. For now, if you care more of the man than the argument, your posture and spirit will exude this. And it should. As Watts concludes, "Let your manner be all candour and gentleness, patient and ready to hear, humbly zealous to inform and be informed; you should be free and pleasant in every answer and bahaviour, rather like well-bred gentlemen in polite conversation, than like noisy and contentious wranglers." [108]

6. *Guard.* Defending and arguing for a position on a topic is more than simply defending the topic or your reputation, if it is this at all. There are other factors at work, and as street-fighting logicians, we must be aware of those other factors. First, there is the sense that truth itself is being defended, not just the truth about the immediate subject. Second, there is the broader context of argument. An argument is occurring and more than likely others are watching and being changed by how that argument takes place. Then, there are at least two people involved, you and your opponent. These two people have distinct personalities, strengths, failings, and some kind of mutual relationship. All of these must be guarded.

First, guard the truth. When it comes to the war *of* words and the war *for* words, we should take no prisoners. Every spoken word should surrender or be eliminated. They should either affirm the given proposition or show themselves obstinate and ex-communicants. Imprisoned and suspended propositions help neither side of the argument. They take up space. They wait in holding, overcrowding the intellectual jail cells and placing a strain on tax-payers. Probation is always an option, but only for the sake of incorporation back into a consistent, functioning worldview. The three laws of thought exude such a fragrance, the sweet and clear fragrance we should hope to smell in all truth claims: a statement is either true or false, there is no in-between; if a statement is true, then it is true; a statement cannot be both true and false at the same time and in the same respect. Therefore, in guarding the truth, be not afraid to interrogate every suspecting citizen, ensuring they give a clear *yes* or *no*. Civil rights activists have more important things to do these days than come for you.

Likewise, be careful of the conclusions you confirm. Understand what you affirm before you simply say, "Yes, and amen." The cost of affirming an idea or doctrine which you have not carefully considered could be your demise in the dispute. Watts says it well. "Watch narrowly in every dispute, that your opponent does not lead you unwarily to grant some principle of the proposition, which will bring with it a fatal consequence, and lead you insensibly into his sentiment…and by this wrong step you will be, as it were, plunged into dangerous errors before you are aware." [109] Again, do not concede a point too quickly. You might be turning over something that undermines all your points. Do not be afraid to say 'I don't know'. As Watts goes on to say, "Remember this short and plain caution of the subtle errors of men. Let a snake but once thrust in his head at some small unguarded fold of your garment, and he will insensibly and unavoidably wind his whole body into your bosom, and give you a pernicious wound." [110]

Second, guard the integrity of disputation. This means guarding both truth and the presentation of that truth. It means knowing when to spot a sophist, even if that sophist is you. "But what could the most presentable waiter do for my thirst by offering precious cups?" Augustine says. "…Fine style does not make something true, nor has a man a wise soul because he has a handsome face and a well-chosen eloquence." [111] Sophistication is not a virtuous badge of Christian rhetoric. In book one of Plato's *Republic*, Thrasemachus is a sophist, and he reveals this in his definition of justice, that justice is whatever is advantageous to the ruler (338c). In this regard, justice is relative to the ruling party. It is regime relative. The sophists were known for their ability to persuade, but not for their ability to search for or teach truth.

Relativists must rely on persuasion and not absolute or necessary truths.

Christians persuade through the dispensing and affirmation of absolute and necessary truths, as well as speech which is agreeable to the Christian frame and working of the Holy Spirit. Christians should love universals, those truths which can be defined, and which must be defined in the same way regardless of time or place. Justice is this kind of thing. In Plato's retelling from the aforementioned scene in his *Republic*, Cleitophon pipes up and proves himself even more of a relativist (340b). As is expected, hungry men don't reach for shape-shifting hamburgers. And no one at Cephalus' house thought Cleitophon's stance harmful or important enough to refute or spend time wrestling with. Thus, no one responded, and he sat down, or walked back outside to see the new god. We are not sure. Plato had better things to write about. And sometimes, there are certain things in a debate we should leave alone due to their harmless anorexia. Augustine further explains the hollow nature of purely fine speech. "…nothing is true merely because it is eloquently said, nor false because the signs coming from the lips make sounds deficient in a sense of style. Again, a statement is not true because it is enunciated in an unpolished idiom, nor false because the words are splendid. Wisdom and foolishness are like food that is nourishing or useless. Whether the words are ornate or not does not decide the issue. Food of either kind can be served in either town or country ware." [112]

Third, guard the person and the relationship. This means guarding yourself against further harm to your own search and inquiry after truth, as well as guarding your neighbor and the relationship between you. Some relationships can handle further argumentation. Others cannot. Certain people can handle being probed deeper. Others cannot. If you truly love the man more than the argument, you will be careful to make the breadth and depth of your dispute proportional to your opponent and the relationship between the both of you. When deciding whether to enter into an argument, consider your purpose. If it is to truly learn from your opponent and conduct a mutually beneficial dialogue, take Watts's advice. "If you would know what sort of companions you should select for the cultivation and advantage of the mind, the general rule is, choose such as, by the brightness of parts, and their diligence in study, or by their superior advancement in learning, or peculiar excellence in any art, science, or accomplishment, divine or human, may be capable of administering to your improvement; and be sure to maintain and keep some due regard to their moral character always, lest while you wander in quest of intellectual gain, you fall into the contagion of irreligion and vice. No wise man would venture into a house infected with the plague, in order to see the finest collections of any virtuoso in England." [113] Just as well, "Let a person have ever so illustrious talents, yet he is not a proper associate for such a purpose, if he lie under any of the following infirmities. 1. If he be exceedingly reserved…2. If he be haughty and proud…3. If he be positive and dogmatical in his own opinions…4. If he be one who always affects to outshine all the company…5. If he be a person of a wiffling and unsteady turn of mind…6. If he be fretful and peevish…7. If he affect wit on all occasions…8. If he carry always about him a sort of craft, and cunning, and disguise…In short, you should avoid the man, in such select conversation, who practices any thing that is unbecoming the character of a sincere, free, and open searcher after truth." [114] There are times when the most beneficial thing is to speak of something edifying, which will neither raise the hairs on anyone's neck nor sweaty the palms. This takes wise discernment, which will be spoken of later.

7. Context. It matters. There is a deeply relational aspect of employing logic, and context is a large part of understanding the relationships involved. Those who employ logic live in a context. Arguments take place in a context. Logic exists within a context. All of these contexts in which you and I and logic live are filled with other beings, other living beings. Some of those are other persons. Some are simply the reality of the natural world. This is perhaps the most important and complex aspects of street-fighting logic. Kant called this 'applied logic' as opposed to 'pure logic'. The former interacts uniquely with psychology while the other interacts uniquely with metaphysics—the branch of philosophy concerned with the study of being. Where and when you argue carries with it its own implications upon the conversation. A presentation about the necessity of abstaining from eating McDonald's french fries will look very different depending on whether you are presenting it to Mr. Potatohead while in a thirty second elevator ride, or to Mrs. Potatohead while she prepares food for a Thanksgiving feast.

When we approach someone in an argument, we must remember that we are engaging with them at a certain place within the story of their life, and within God's story. They are at a particular point in their day, probably partaking in particular tasks, either vocational or leisurely. Your opponent is on a journey. Your argument takes place within a space-time continuum. This space-time continuum is the kind of thing that has a past, present, and future. In an argument, you are in that person's present. Argue in such a way that the truths they have learned in their past will interact with the truths you are presenting, and that the truths you are presenting will give them something to ponder throughout the experiences in their future. And consider your future relationship with this person, that the topic at hand has potential to be revisited time and again between you and your opponent. Your goal is not to change their past or control their future, because you can do neither. Your goal is to be faithful in the present and consider its relation to *this* person's past and *this* person's anticipated future.

Likewise, just as we are engaging with our opponent at a certain point in the story of their life, we are engaging with them at a certain point in the story of our life. That is to say, both of us have come to live and move and have our being as characters on this particular stage and within this particular plot sequence. Whatever their claims may be on a subject, and whatever that subject may be, they have arrived at this conclusion in story-fashion. This means that in order for us to be understood, we must seek to understand. This also means that they may not have a systematic argument for their conclusion on the subject. It is getting to be a rare occasion that someone has considered how one conclusion on a particular subject interacts and coincides with the rest of their worldview, even on the most basic topics. In other words, people are more and more unable to synthesize and coherently hold the truth-claims they have come to hold. There are multiple reasons for this: the capacity of the common intelligence, the apathy of the common heart, and the sin of the common man. Either way, this person before you is a living story, not a body bag of propositions.

First, pull the nuances needed to argue well from your immediate surroundings. This is part of knowing that you are always in God's story and set upon a wonderful stage, as stated earlier. At all times and in all places you are surrounded by one of two different designs, maybe both simultaneously. You are always surrounded by the natural world, creation, *creatio ex nihilo*. Even among a concrete playground which extends for miles, your body reflects the making of the natural world. In this way, you can never be less than a natural man, endowed with those gifts, abilities and boundaries that all natural men have. You are also surrounded by the work of human hands, sub-creation, *creatio ex materia*; this being an outplaying of our being made in the image of God. God is a creator. He created a world. He created a story. He created characters and plots. In retaining His image, we share in his desire and ability to create a world around us. Thus, architects, designers and craftsmen will always be needed in any human society. Take your cues from these two surroundings. Use these as possible metaphors to drive home a point, or raise a question which could more readily render your opponent's claim unsound. Again, observation is a powerful tool. And real-time observation will make a lively claim upon the hearer. You can use the immediate, material world to bring to mind a more metaphysical claim. As John Calvin states, "In short, the many pre-eminent gifts with which the human mind is endowed proclaim that something divine has been engraved upon it; all these are testimonies of an immortal essence. For the sense perception inhering in brute animals does not go beyond the body, or at least extends no farther than to material things presented to it. But the nimbleness of the human mind in searching out heaven and earth and the secrets of nature, and when all ages have been compassed by its understanding and memory, in arranging each thing in its proper order, and in inferring future events from past, clearly shows that there lies hidden in man something separate from the body. With our intelligence we conceive the invisible God and the angels, something the body can by no means do. We grasp things that are right, just, and honorable, which are hidden to the bodily senses." [115]

Second, do not just pull from your context in order to win the argument. Pull from your context in order to know when to cease arguing, or even which presentation of this argument is best for the present situation. Again, a thirty-second elevator ride on the sovereignty of God will look quite different than a sit-down discussion over coffee. Both could happen. And both could be teachable moments. Both could also end horribly if not handled according to their respective potentials and limitations.

Context not only includes the immediate surroundings, but your immediate opponent. Are you arguing with your mom? Your brother? Your teacher? An elder at the church? How old are you? How old are they? What does God say about their relationship to you and how you should interact according to that relationship? As Watts explains, "A young man, in the presence of his elders, should rather hear and attend, and weigh the arguments which are brought for proof or refutation of any doubtful proposition: and when it is your turn to speak, propose your thoughts rather in the way of inquiry. By this means your mind will be kept in a fitter temper to receive truth..." [116] Likewise, read the context of the argument, the broader purpose for the argument's existence. "Do not bring your warm party spirit into a free conversation which is designed for mutual improvement in the search of truth." [117] Two years of logic or thirty-five gives us no grounds to argue with the Wal-Mart cashier of the 20-items-or-less-line how the person in front of us has 22 items, and thus has violated some kind of social code. We should likewise not go argue with the Wal-Mart manager that the sign should actually read "20 items or fewer!" and not "20 items or less," for "less" is not for objects able to be quantified. A man can have less money; he can have fewer dollars. To pick these kinds of fights would not prove you have learned to argue. On the contrary, you have learned to be a disrespectful prig.

Just as well, part of the context of the dispute must account for sin, even if that is the topic of argument. Your opponent's journey, as does yours, includes original sin, potential for present sin, and the inevitability of past and future sin. This affects the reasoning process. It always has. Because we are whole creatures, persons rather than processing units, our parts work together organically, and quite mysteriously. Because our fallen nature is not marginalized to one part of our lives and not another, our arguments need to account for this. This means we must have patience, and seek to convey a truth in as many ways as possible, knowing that the hard heart is often a stubborn patient, and the depraved mind does its bidding. Augustine speaks clearly of this. "Just as crimes occur when the mind's motive force, which gives the impetus for action, is corrupt and asserts itself in an insolent and disturbed way, and as vicious acts occur if obsession has captured the mind's affective part which is at the root of the impulse to carnal pleasures, so also errors and false opinions contaminate life if the reasoning mind is itself flawed…For I did not know that the soul needs to be enlightened by light from outside itself, so that it can participate in truth, because it is not itself the nature of truth." [118] A soft answer really does turn away wrath (Prov. 15:1), and the absence of wrath allows for the presence of receptivity.

So, in short, rationality is always situated rationality. It is situated in time and among particular persons. It is situated in a peculiar context of space and time that will never occur again. And this brings with every dispute certain uniqueness. It should bring to it a certain love for the mystery and art of belief and action, which cannot be quantified as easily as some would have us think. Nicholas Wolterstorff, in *Faith and Rationality*, superbly explains this. His words are worth quoting at length:

"So the full picture that emerges is something like this: we each have a variety of belief dispositions, some of which we share with all normal, mature human beings, some of which we do not; some of which we have as part of our native endowment, some of which are the result of one and another form of conditioning, and probably some of which are the result of having resolved to resist the workings of some native or conditioned disposition. In addition, we each have a variety of capacities for governing the workings of these dispositions. To some extent it is in our power to determine whether a certain (sort of) triggering event for a disposition will occur. And to some extent it is in our power to determine whether the disposition will be activated even if an event does not occur which characteristically would activate it. Perhaps we also have the capacity in certain (relatively rare) circumstances to *decide* whether to believe something.

It must be clearly noted that rationality, thus, conceived, is in good measure person specific and situation specific. When I was young, there were things which it was rational for me to believe which now, when I am older, it is no longer rational for me to believe. And for a person reared in a traditional tribal society who never comes into contact with another society or culture, there will be things rational to believe which for me, a member of the modern Western intelligentsia, would not be rational to believe. Rationality of belief can only be determined in context – historical and social contexts, and, even more narrowly, personal context. It has long been the habit of philosophers to ask in abstract, nonspecific fashion whether it is rational to believe that God exists, whether it is rational to believe that there is an external world, whether it is rational to believe that there are other persons, and so on. Mountains of confusion have resulted. The proper question is always and only whether it is rational for this or that particular person in this or that situation, or for a person of this or that particular type in this or that type of situation, to believe so-and-so. Rationality is always *situated* rationally." [119]

In the end, disputation, and the proper use of street-fighting logic, is about persons. Aristotle reminds us. "...experience is knowledge of individuals, art of universals, and actions and productions are all connected with the individual; for the physician does not cure *man*, except in an incidental way, but Callias or Socrates or some other called by some such individual name, who happens to be a man. If, then, a man has the theory without the experience, and recognizes the universal but does not know the individual included in this, he will often fail to cure; for it is the individual that is to be cured." [120]

8. Shrewdness. Be shrewd as serpents in your argument, in both form and content. All arguments have a structure and all arguments contain content. In other words, all arguments are about something and present a truth or falsity in a particular way about that thing. In order to be shrewd about both the structure and content of your argument and your opponent's, you need to become good at what has been mentioned thus far in this chapter. Shrewdness in street-fighting logic is the ability to master all that has been written up to now. It is also the ability to recognize foundational problems in adversarial dialogue. Question at least, and maybe at most, the validity of the argument. If valid, consider whether one of the premises is false, making the argument unsound. Once you have identified a false premise, and have even gotten them to a point of realizing the plausibility of it being false, argue in such a way that increases the plausibility of a true premise replacing the false. Even if they do not immediately concede your proposed premise, encourage them to think about it and the implications of it. Again, leave them with a question to consider. As Watts says of this subject, "When you are engaged in a dispute with a person of very different principles from yourself, and you cannot find any ready way to prevail with him to embrace the truth by principles which you both freely acknowledge, you may fairly make use of his own principles to show him his mistake, and thus convince or silence him from his own concessions." [121] It is like using someone's weight against them in a wrestling match. Be resourceful.

Similarly, speak with people as the people they are. Watts explains, "If you happen to be in company with a merchant or sailor, a farmer or mercantile, a milk-maid or a spinster, lead them into a discourse of the matters of their own peculiar province or profession; for every one knows or should know, their own business best. In this sense a common mechanic is wiser than the philosopher. By this means you may gain some improvement of knowledge from every one you meet...A free and general conversation with men of very various countries, and of different parties, opinions, and practices, so far as it may be done safely, is of excellent use to undeceive us in many wrong judgments which we may have framed, and to lead us into juster thoughts." [122] Not only will you gain a deeper and wider knowledge of many fields, but you will, by friendship and grace, upon the rise of some disputation, gain a listening ear and set a cordial stage for understanding your opponent. In Christian love, you can choose metaphors, arguments and examples which would most accord with the previous knowledge which they already hold. This will prove most beneficial as it is in bad taste to argue with an elderly florist the same way and with the same terms you would a sprite academic. Shrewdness and context are not mutually exclusive. And even tact-in-play could be training for future bouts.

Be shrewd in the path of argument you choose, not simply what you say. G.K. Chesterton said, "To show that a faith or a philosophy is true from every standpoint would be too big an undertaking even for a much bigger book than this; it is necessary to follow one path of argument…" [123] Chesterton is encouraging us to choose an angle in an argument. When we attempt to prove our argument, don't attempt to prove it proper from every angle. Likewise, when we determine our opponent's position to be worthy of confrontation, we need not prove its inability in every way. Choose the best route, the best angle, by which to prove your opponent's position untenable. When choosing an angle, be wise with your choice, perhaps choosing an angle which accounts for other angles such that felling that wall would have the logical consequence of felling three subsequent and adjoining walls. In short, there may be one-hundred arguments to support the same conclusion; a well-trained street-fighting logician need only present one argument, the best and most prudent argument, in order to fulfill one's goal in convincing an opponent.

9. *Innocence.* Be as innocent as doves, and live above reproach during and outside times of dispute. Notice how I did not say "Play nice." Kindness and niceness are two quite different virtues, if niceness is a virtue at all. I agree with C.S. Lewis. "God did not come to make us nice men but new men." Nice guys are bad arguers, and even worse evangelists. Nowhere in Scripture are we as Christians called to be nice. We are called to be kind, loving, gentle, longsuffering, submissive, empathetic, shrewd, holy, courageous, speakers of truth and protectors of the innocent. But nice? No. Niceness is a false humility. It is a false virtue. Nice is often synonymous with another modern false virtue: tolerance. 'Nice' is what parents tell their young boys they should be when every other parenting technique does not work. Nice is not a Christian virtue. It is a humanistic façade, at best. Thus, *innocence and love* are not equivalent to *nice little boys and girls*. Innocence and love are for those who want to be faithful in

applying good logic to everyday scenarios; the kind of scenarios that are organic, humbling and God-glorifying. So, niceness will not do the job, or even get you the best kinds of jobs. It takes more than that. It takes strategy. Not the nice kind of strategy; the biblical kind; the kind that truly renders you innocent in the sight of both man and God. The first step to innocence in argument is to, "...know that it is nothing but truth constrains you to oppose him; and let that difference be always expressed in few, and civil, and chosen words, such as may give the least offence." [124]

First, being innocent does not mean being perfect. Sins wound. Deep sins wound deeply. Social sins wound socially. And personal sins are never private. Burned bridges do not just dissipate into thin air. They fall into the river below which will eventually become drinking water for the surrounding communities, maybe even your own. Before they fall, make it right. Be able to say "I am sorry" if you really offended, truly sinned, not just stepped on their toes, which could sometimes be a good thing if their toes were on fire. If you offend in word, say "I'm sorry". If you offend in deed, act accordingly. And remember that your body language is a part of your rhetoric. In many ways, your body language can be a kind of argument in itself. Let both your speech and your body language be seasoned with salt. Let your truth be seasoned with grace. Look for places to give soft answers. It turns away wrath. And be prepared to enact Watts's advice. "Whensoever, therefore, any unhappy word shall arise in company, that might give you a reasonable disgust, quash the rising resentment, be it ever so just, and command your soul and your tongue into silence, lest you cancel the hopes of all improvement for that hour, and transform the learned conversation into the mean and vulgar form of reproaches and railing. The man who began to break the peace in such a society, will fall under the shame and conviction of such a silent reproof, if he has any thing ingenuous about him. If this should not be sufficient, let a grave admonition, or a soft and gentle turn of wit, with an air of pleasantry, give the warm disputer an occasion to stop the progress of his indecent fire, if not to retract the indecency, and quench the flame." [125] The 18th century Puritan theologian Jonathan Edwards made three resolutions we all would do well to keep:

"Resolution #58. Resolved, Not only to refrain from an air of dislike, fretfulness, and anger in conversation, but to exhibit an air of love, cheerfulness, and benignity. May 27, and July 13, 1723"

"Resolution #66. Resolved, That I will endeavour always to keep a benign aspect, and air of acting and speaking, in all places, and in all companies, except it should so happen that duty requires otherwise."

"Resolution #70. Let there be something of benevolence in all that I speak. Aug. 17, 1723."

Second, innocence is not based on the judgment of man, but the judgment of God. In any argument, keep your hands clean. You cannot live your life trying to please every man and God. As Solon said, "In great affairs, you cannot please all parties." It is improbable to please all men. Outside of Christ, it is impossible to please God. It is only those who are in Christ who realize that the latter supersedes the former. So, please God and let those who know God be pleased with you. The others are going to find something to complain about anyway. Lewis knew this well. "There comes of course a degree of evil against which a protest will have to be made, however little chance it has of success. There are cheery agreements in cynicism or brutality which one must contract out of unambiguously. If it can't be done without seeming priggish, then priggish we must seem. For what really matters is not seeming but being a prig...As for the mere seeming – well, though it is very bad to be a prig, there are social atmospheres so foul that in them it is almost an alarming symptom if a man has never been called one. Just in the same way, though pedantry is a folly and snobbery a vice, yet there are circles in which only a man indifferent to all accuracy will escape being called a pedant, and others where manners are so coarse, flashy and shameless that a man (whatsoever his social position) of any natural good taste will be called a snob." [126]

10. Stop and Start. The fullness of an idea or a topic cannot be captured by the intellect alone. This will be explained more fully in the coming chapter. But there must be a word spoken here because of its pertinence to strategy. As has been said before, being a good street-fighting logician is as much about knowing when and what not to say as it is about knowing when and what to say. As Jasper Hopkins once said in his *Prolegomena to Nicholas of Cusa's Conception of the Relationship of Faith and Reason*, "The fanatic is someone who believes in such a way that no evidence, no further reflection, no new consideration will lead him to abandon or even to modify his view. Perhaps Winston Churchill said it right when he defined a fanatic as an individual who *cannot* change his mind and who *will not* change the subject." [127] A fanatic is the worst kind of debater because he is not in it for the sake of what is true, but rather his own preconceived notions. And to think we are not prone to fanaticism is to think too highly of ourselves. "It is great men," Lewis said, "potential saints, not little men, who become merciless fanatics." [128] So, part of avoiding fanaticism is knowing when to stop, to change the subject, or at least come up for air, and allow your opponent to do the same. When we are repeating ourselves, like fanatics tend to do, either we are afraid to take the next step—or just do not know how—or we are indulging someone's vanities, probably our own.

Avoiding fanaticism is also about holding our convictions proportionate to their importance for a faithful life in Christ. Eating organic food or not is a minor issue, if it is an issue at all, and one which is much less significant than our green-thumbed neighbor may portray. Likewise, your strength of conviction on a topic should be proportional to the work and labor you have done to get there. Do not hold with a tightly clinched fist anything that a good night's sleep on your part may remedy. And don't respond to anything that a good night's rest on their part will dispel.

Another aspect of knowing when to stop the argument is knowing the boundaries of dialectic. Again, more on this later, but a word here is necessary. As Christians, we are whole men. We are incarnate beings. To separate our minds from the rest of our bodies, passions, and celebrations would be a false dichotomy. Such dualism is against the Christian Scriptures and against the Church's historical stance on the essence of man. If most logic texts miss any point by a wide margin, it is this one. Most logic texts are written in and from a post-Enlightenment, worldview, which creates an unrealistic dualism. As Lewis explains this in historical terms, "The Jews were not, like the Greeks, an analytical and logical people; indeed, except the Greeks, no ancient peoples were." [129] The festal and analytic are not opposed. They are both sharpened and clarified by the presence of the other. When dialectic fails (and often it will), use story, song, or silence to convey your point.

To argue well is a good desire, a noble chase. We ought to be as masterful at it as we can become this side of heaven. And this mastery consists of knowing the limits to argumentation, when to stop. For now and the rest of our lives, no matter how proficient one may become at reasonably arguing an atheist off his love of non-God, it will maintain that one's artwork may be the best strategy. This is so because art deals primarily in the realm of beauty, of story, which does not mean it avoids truth. And these two disciplines, beauty and story, are among the only that will discipline the rationalistic atheist, precisely because they do not properly understand reason. Art and story will soften his heart faster than a rationalistic argument against his rationalism. It will do to him what an expansive field of wild daisies does to a young girl, or what a distant stampede of wild, Wyoming stallions does to a young boy. It will not make him forget he is man. Rather, it will make him realize he is nothing more than man.

As an albeit brief defense of narrative and poetic knowledge, Louise Cowan states in the introduction to her *Invitation to the Classics*, "Not until a literary work of art awakened my imaginative faculties could the possibility of a larger context than reason alone engage my mind. I had been expecting logical proof of something one was intended to recognize. What was needed was a way of seeing. I had to be transformed in the way that literature transforms – by story, image, symbol – before I could *see* the simple truths of the gospel. Above all else this seems to me the chief value of what we call the classics: they summon us to belief. They seize our imaginations and make us *commit ourselves to the self-evident*, which we have forgotten how to recognize." [130] There is enough here to unpack for many more pages, which could turn into many more books. But what is most important to point out for our current project is just how someone's apprehension of an idea, or ascent to a proposition, takes more than dialectical conversation. It takes more than just valid syllogisms proven time and again. A trust in and love for poetic knowledge is a necessary component to the street-fighting logician. In this way, we no longer become logicians, but poets and artists. Even in maintaining as strictly as possible our logical nature, we must concede that there is a deep reliance upon the poetic. As the authors of *Classical Education and the Homeschool* state, "But it's not only moral judgments that suffer from a defective imagination. Plain reasoning does too. One of the common myths about logic is that it can free us from that 'nasty' world of metaphor and imagination. Almost every logic text goes to some pains to explain why metaphor has to be reduced or exiled from logical discourse. Logic can't handle figurative language, so it has to be reduced to the literal…The irony is, of course, that logic itself grows out of some very basic metaphors that quickly get forgotten…All of morality and reasoning involve imagination and metaphor. They can't get off the ground without it. And we learn to exercise our imaginations in stories – fiction and fantasy and fairy tales most tellingly." [131]

As Christians, this kind of reality must be clear and present. After all, the foundation for our faith is the testimony of a work of literature, which is hardly a systemic compilation of formal arguments. The presence and pertinence of this piece of literature greatly affects how we understand the boundaries of reason. Augustine explains this well. "So since we were too weak to discover the truth by pure reasoning and therefore needed the authority of the sacred writings, I now began to believe that you would never have conferred such preeminent authority on the scripture, now diffused through all lands, unless you had willed that it would be a means of coming to faith in you and a means of seeking to know you." [132]

In his introduction to *Orthodoxy*, Chesterton explains his style in a similar manner, "…I have attempted in a vague and personal way, in a set of mental pictures rather than in a series of deductions, to state the philosophy in which I have come to believe." [133] And how can we have a defense of poesy without the words of Sir Philip Sidney. "Anger, the Stoics said, was short madness: let but Sophocles bring you Ajax on stage, killing or whipping sheep and oxen thinking them the army of the Greeks with their chieftains Agamemnon and Menelaus, and tell me if you have not a more familiar insight into anger than finding in the schoolmen his genus and difference... For the question is, whether the feigned image of poetry or the regular instruction of philosophy hath the more force in teaching...I say the philosophers teacheth, but he teacheth obscurely, so as the learned only can understand him: that is to say, he teacheth them that are already taught. But the poet is the food for the tenderest stomachs; the poet is indeed the right popular philosopher. Whereof Aesop's tales give good proof, whose pretty allegories, stealing under the formal tales of beasts, make many, more beastly than beasts, begin to hear the sound of virtue from these dumb speakers." [134] For now, and for the present purpose, enough has been said on where deductive reasoning may end and poetic delight begin. Be not afraid to have this nearby in your arsenal.

As for song, its mysterious impact is the same we find in all poetry. Song, as a kind of poetry, resonates with us in a fuller sense. It hits our bones. It appeals to our souls. It does so with a rhythm and mood that is often not found in the cold, philosophical dialogue of the logicians. The Ancients knew this, and I believe we still have it deep within us, though our broader society has tended toward the analytic and scientific as the primary method of determining what is true, good, and beautiful. I am reminded of the scene in the movie *Amazing Grace* when Wilberforce's character stands on the table among the gambling politicians and begins singing Newton's "Amazing Grace". I am also reminded of a story I once heard of a professor who was giving a reasoned defense for Christianity in a college classroom. A young man in the front row raised his hand and said, "I believe none of what you have said." The student remained standing, putting his non-theistic beliefs out front. When he was done, the professor gave a simple reply: "Then please, sir, sing to me of your atheism and I will be done with my talk. Sing for all of us, loudly." There was silence. The class waited. Embarrassed, the student sat down. As Tchaikovsky said, "When words fail, we have music."

Even still, when words reach their extent, we also have silence. As John Boy states in the opening episode of season one of *The Waltons*, "The power of the pen may be great, but in love it has failed me. Tomorrow I plan action." Though his action was not one of silence, ours could very well be. And by actually living by this, we eventually find Lewis's words true, "Silence is a good refuge." [135] And hear Ignatius to the Ephesians, "It is better for a man to be silent and be [a Christian], than to talk and not be one."

With that said of strategy, we segue into our next section: the goal of street-fighting logic, along with the deep and wide limitations of logic.

Focus Questions.
1. What is strategy?
2. What are the ten strategic points mentioned in this chapter?
3. Which of the ten main points in the chapter is easiest for you? Which is most difficult?
4. What is the Socratic method, and how can it be particularly effective?
5. Why is it best for one to avoid their own "ruffled feathers" during a debate?
6. What does it mean to be fair in an argument?
7. When would silence be the best strategy in a debate?
8. If there was to be an 11th point to strategy, what would it be?

Exercises.
1. Choose a hot topic for debate. Choose a context (setting). Choose two characters. Write a 350-400 word dialogue where one person clearly breaks three of the ten points from this chapter and the other person does not.
2. Have a friend or stranger spend five minutes talking about their favorite vacation memory. Without taking notes, remember the main point. Go home and write down those main points. Write down as much detail as you can remember.

Chapter 4
The Goal

"*Resolved*, to examine carefully and constantly, what that one thing in me is, which causes me in the least to doubt of the love of God; and so direct all my forces against it." Jonathan Edwards, *70 Resolutions*.

"Nevertheless, to praise you is the desire of man, a little piece of your creation. You stir man to take pleasure in praising you, because you have made us for yourself, and our heart is restless until it rests in you." Augustine[136]

"I doubt if your interests get less intellectual as you become more deeply involved in the Church, but what will happen is that the intellect will take its place in a large context and will cease to be tyrannical, if it has been – and when there is nothing over the intellect it usually is tyrannical. Anyways, the mind serves best when it's anchored in the word of God. There is no danger then of becoming an intellectual without integrity." Flannery O'Connor[137]

"The person who knows the truth knows it, and he who knows it knows eternity." Augustine[138]

"Here we have a paradox of faith: that it is reasonable to believe what reason tells us it is unreasonable to believe – that it is reasonable to believe that there is truth which exceeds the grasp of reason." Jasper Hopkins[139]

"It is no use saying he is the Alpha and Omega, the beginning and the end, the Lord of all things, if he is not the Lord of my whole unified intellectual life. I am false or confused if I sing about Christ's lordship and contrive to retain areas of my own life that are autonomous." Francis Schaeffer[140]

"One can only find truth with logic if you have already found truth without it." G.K. Chesterton, *Daily News*, 1905

The ends are important for determining the means. This goes for common affairs in life as well as grand ones. For example, in a philosophy of education, our vision for what man *should be*, or at least what an educated man should be, would determine *how* we make him this way. If we think an educated man is simply another tool in the everyday grind of capitalism, we will set up our education systems to produce the finest cog in the wheel; so we have. If we believe he is to be simply an overindulged ape that has gone further than his predecessors in the evolutionary process, we will set up our education systems to produce the most advanced ape this planet has ever witnessed; so we have. Our streets are covered with primates donning hair gel and Armani. Fortunately, both of these assumptions about education and its end are wrong. Unfortunately, most of our modern philosophies of education think they are right, at least functionally. The same goes with arguments.

Those who argue from a biblical standard are not to be peace-makers in the "let's all just be friends" kind of way. At the same time, we should not be argumentative in the "I did it my way" kind of routine. As Christians who employ good logic, we should seek to make peace, but in the right way and between the right people. Some people *should* be your enemies. If they are not, you are not living properly. Jesus, the most loving person to ever take on human form, was hated, mocked, slandered, and eventually killed…by his enemies.

So, then what is the goal of street-fighting logic? Why engage in street-fighting logic and how? With whom should I engage? When should I engage? What is the goal of my engagement? These questions must be supported by a kind of wisdom that often only comes with age and lots of learning-on-the-job lessons. Still, especially for the younger readers but certainly for all readers, we would do well to begin considering the answers to these questions now. They are questions that we can habitually ask ourselves, and questions we will learn how to more appropriately answer as we grow in interacting with people and picking up on interpersonal and social clues. But to answer concisely, the answer to the above questions is simple: the Christian use of logic should always be to speak truth into a messy world full of messy lives, pleasing man and glorifying God. As Peter Kreeft puts it, "This power of logic is rightly used to win the truth and defeat error; it is wrongly used to win the argument and defeat your opponent." [141]

Before engaging in any argument, we would do well to ask two questions: Why am I choosing to engage in an argument with this person? Why am I choosing to engage in *this* argument? If we were honest, some common answers to these two questions would be something like, "Because I am winning the argument and I sound so smart!" or "Because I'm trying to impress my friend who is with me." or "Because I really want to try this logic stuff out and show how well Christians really can argue." The list could go on. Your ability to argue well is no more important than your motivations to argue at all. If you can present an air-tight, Aristotle-befuddling argument, yet you are nothing more than a Sophisticated relativist out to prove his own worth, then you are no better than someone who knows not a bit of logic. In fact, you are worse for having taken something so wonderful and made it a slave to your selfish gain. If we are going to be faithful street-fighting logicians, we must have a good understanding of the goal of argument.

The scandal of the educated mind is that we come to believe we are educated, that we have harnessed Truth in nicely bound pages and can sell it via the local street-vendor for twice its production cost. But Truth is not so easily tamed, and knowledge enjoys puffing up. Pride is an ever-lurking foe for the one who seeks to know, and yet slides into a state of losing the acknowledgment of both the mysterious and unknowable. Therefore, one of the goals of the street-fighting logician is to understand the limits of human reason in conveying and defending truth. Likewise, we should rightly be seeking to understand who man is, and how he must come to be truly happy in this life.

Along the same lines of both goals, blinded eyes cannot see light no matter how brightly you shine it. Another way of saying this is that changing the hue of the painting does not show the man with rose-colored glasses the true color of the painting. Corpses cannot be shaken to life. Part of knowing when to stop and when to continue is to know the capacity of your opponent. "Truth may exist while people reject it; and people may in turn create all types of falsehoods and call them truth. These activities represent fallen man's desperate attempts to impute his own truth instead of God's." [142] Truth can stare people in the face, even heal them and talk with them, and they still mistake it as a petty thief. Light makes truth. Well, light doesn't *make* the truth. It makes the element of 'presencing' the truth. Truth is the manifestation of reality to the mind, and this ability and light to agree with reality must be given from without. As whole beings with a body, mind, and soul, we must realize there are both intellectual roadblocks and moral roadblocks for the street-fighting logician in convincing his opponent of even the most mundane truths, and especially the most fantastic ones.

As was mentioned in the previous chapter, argument should not only be anthropocentric, in the sense that the life and soul of your opponent is more important than your theoretical stance on an issue, but it should also be Christocentric, in the sense that, as *Westminster Confession of Faith* states, the chief end of man is to glorify God and enjoy him forever. Often, street-fighting logic has little to do with the formal verdict of the argument. Formal debate cares deeply about the final verdict, because there will be one. But the common confrontations of street-fighting logic are more about imparting a certain kind of story into an otherwise confused and unclear worldview. Street-fighting logic is the tweaking of lenses, the presentation of a different world, even on this particular subject, in which the person could live and move and have his being. Thus, arguments—a set of statements, two or more of those statements supporting the other—are not necessarily for winning; they are for presenting truth in all its brilliance and clarity, in all of its cut, clarity, color, and carat to your opponent at this time in their story. To think that arguments are for winning is to think that words are some kind of competition. Again, in doing this, we make the same mistake as the Sophists. Words become a power-grab. We place ourselves and our reputation at the center of the goal. The only prize to be found cannot be issued by human hands, but by the hands of Him who gives to each breath the ability to present propositions and deny someone else's. And to reiterate, we must therefore understand both the intentions and extensions of dialectic. We must understand the role of dialectic and its limitations in loving our neighbor and showing the glory of the Lord, who is the *logos*.

All that has been said so far may be summarized in this: win the argument and win the man. There is such a thing as winning the argument and losing the man. This is when you are logically infallible though personably wretched—careful with your mind but careless with your opponent's soul. There is also such a thing as losing the argument and winning the man. This is the other ditch, the opposite problem. Here you are logically careless, though sincere with your fallacies. As Christians we must avoid both errors. We must reason well and love our neighbor. Peter Kreeft in his *Socratic* Logic identifies this as a material, or informal, fallacy. " 'Winning the argument but losing the arguer' means ignoring the personal, psychological factor and ending up being distrusted and treated as an enemy or a threat by the person you wanted to persuade." He continues: "Both personal and interpersonal dimensions are necessary as two parts of all interpersonal argument, and neither one can make up for the lack of the other." [143]

As referenced in the first chapter, Peter Kreeft begins his *Socratic Logic* with thirteen answers to the question "What good is logic?" His ninth answer is "Defining logic's limits. Does logic have limits? Yes, but we need logic to recognize and define logic's limits." Answer twelve reads, "Certainty. Logic has 'outer limits'; there are many things it can't give you. But logic has no 'inner limits': like math, it never breaks down." Kreeft goes on to give a brief list of that which sits outside the outer limits of logic: humor, feeling, and intuition—all non-logical factors of understanding.

While that which sits outside the range of logic has been called many things, perhaps it is most appropriately called poetic knowledge, as opposed to what is often called speculative or analytic knowledge—the knowledge of the philosopher and the scientist. Non-speculative knowledge, according to the 20th century Catholic French philosopher Jacques Maritain who followed in Aquinas's *from*

footsteps, is most accurately called *inclination*—sympathy, congeniality, and connaturality. This inclination falls into three kinds for Maritain: moral knowledge (of the virtuous man), mystical knowledge (of the contemplative), and poetic knowledge (non-conceptual knowledge by the artist). Poetic knowledge in particular is the knowledge which comes by making. It is "...the intrinsic moment of contemplation form which creation emanates...Poetic knowledge is non-conceptual and non-rational knowledge; it is born in the preconscious life of the intellect, and it is essentially an obscure revelation both of the subjectivity of the poet and of some flash of reality coming together out of sleep in one single awakening." [144]

James Taylor, author and professor, compiles an impressive text on the philosophy and history of poetic knowledge in *Poetic Knowledge*. "First of all," he begins, "poetic knowledge is not necessarily a knowledge of poetry but rather a poetic (a sensory-emotional) experience of reality...it is not strictly speaking a knowledge of poems, but a spontaneous act of the external and internal senses with the intellect, integrated and whole, rather than an act associated with the powers of analytical reasoning." [145] That is to say, poetic knowledge is a method of epistemology which allows for a particular kind of knowing, and this method of knowing results not from us being *homo sapiens* (man as thinker), but from us being *homo faber* (man as maker), *homo adorans* (man as worshipper), and *homo liturgicus* (man as lover or desirer). This means that reason is always narratival reason, contextualized and decorated by the whole man. Thus, street-fighting logic, as taking place amidst the commoners, is always radiating with the fullness of man in the lived body. It is likewise a kind of leisure, or even play, which sets the stage for poetic knowledge. Josef Pieper in *Leisure as the Basis of Culture* states, "...the essence of knowing would lie, not in the effort of thought as such, but in the grasp of the being of things, in the discovery of reality." [146] In distinguishing the analytic paradigm from the poetic paradigm, N.D and Douglas Wilson state in their *Rhetoric Companion*, "[The analytic paradigm] assumes that every intellectual problem has a solution when the following criteria, which are necessary to the method, are employed in finding that solution. The method requires *precision*; it requires *quantification*; it requires *abstraction*; and the method requires *direct correlation*...In contrast, we have the poetic paradigm. The approach of poetry – which includes the metaphor, simile, personification, etc. – requires *imprecision;* it requires *qualification;* it uses *concrete images;* and the approach requires *oblique correlation.* And, ironically, it also helps communicate more accurately." [147] Even when employing the analytical, the formal rules of argument, we ought not attempt to escape the poetic. When one presents something analytically, with a strong cerebral stench, to be most effective he must do so poetically. That is to say, even when we argue analytically, inductively and deductively, we argue not with machines but with humans, and this means we must take into account the imagination and the desires, the *ordo amoris.*

In Western tradition, it is noteworthy that this discussion has surfaced time and again, and it is likewise noteworthy to consider our early frames as humans. Upon entering the world, we live poetically before we live rationally. We live festively before we live discursively. And even as we move into a more dialectical interaction with the world and one another, we remain creatures of intuition, of assumed rather than proved knowledge, assumed with warrant on the basis of reliable authority. Poetic knowledge is not a knowledge that is contra-logic. It is a knowledge that is para-logic.

The Perverted Intellect

As much as we in the classical Christian tradition love the life of the mind, and as much as I have esteemed and will continue to esteem the necessary presence of a logic course within any healthy education, there must be something further said of its limits. The best logicians are the ones who understand the inherent limitations of reason. The world is splattered with great mysteries, things that logic – as we know it in its academic form – will never be able to touch. In dealing specifically with the Christian gospel, man's reasoning faculties were never intended to replace Christ. Some have maintained that reason alone can bring man into a right relationship with his neighbor and whatever divine being may exist. This is faulty. This is a kind of worldview that is dominating the West, and something we as Christian scholars must be prepared to answer. It is called rational*ism*. Valid arguments with faulty basic beliefs lead only to reading Shakespeare while tightening your own shackles. Hence, with the wrong kind of understanding of logic, we do not partake in a liberal education, one that frees, but one that enslaves us more to our passions and self-deceiving desires. As Christians, we are not slaves to reason. The claims of Christianity are inconsistent with those of rationalism. This is so, as John Calvin rightly states, because "Our reason is overwhelmed by so many forms of deceptions, is subject to so many errors, dashes against so many obstacles, is caught in so many difficulties, that it is far from directing us aright." [148] Still, to rightly appraise the goal of reasonable arguments, and the strategy we are to use, we must understand the extreme positions others have taken concerning logic: rationalism and irrationalism, or intellectualism and anti-intellectualism.

Spend one day in the halls of a public school or many private schools and you will realize that our culture as a whole has done nearly everything but grow in a centralized love for the academic community. 'The nerd' is much less popular among the youth of America than 'the jock.' Modern films portray it and the idea is prevalent among the major media our culture uses to express itself. I do understand there are exceptions. But this is most certainly the general rule today. The deep studier is much more marginalized and disregarded than the popular cheerleader, movie-star or frat hero. American youth are more concerned with video games and sports practice than community and truth. Dinner with an author or theologian is much less desired than a sweatband from an NFL quarterback. Even at universities and colleges, professors are mostly sought after if they are 'an easy A' or if they are 'cool'. The professor is often avoided if he is 'hard' or 'challenging'. I call this particular trend 'pupil selectivity from pupil irresponsibility'.

An important aspect of scholarship is to challenge and build one's mind with a proper worldview and practice of human disciplines, to make the student more fully human. It should be designed to be intentionally formational. Any curriculum which, or student in academia who, does not hope for this sort of environment is wholly hurting themselves and their topics of study. It is one of the worst kinds of deceits the intellectual community has ever known: the weakening of both curriculum and challenge at the expense of uninformed people. Whether it is the university or the student that exhibits this behavior—or of course the third and most probable option of both—is not the main focus here. Whether it is the university that has neglected the proper formation of the intellect, or society which chooses to nominally engage in a great system—or again, the third option of both—is not the greatest problem. The greatest problem is that it *has* happened, and currently *is* happening.

Many present-day scholars have referred to this phenomenon as 'anti-intellectualism'. Not only has anti-intellectualism happened in our secular society, but it has festered its way into the Christian community. As J.P. Moreland reflects on its ecclesial affects, he states, "Sadly, emerging anti-intellectualism in the church created a lack of readiness for the widespread intellectual assault on Christianity...that was launched on three major areas: Philosophical ideas from Europe...German higher criticism of the Bible...[and] Darwinian evolution." [149]

Moreland then goes on to critique the specific ways present-day Christianity in the west, and its global impact, has been affected by this shift. While using the analogy from Matthew chapter five, he concludes that inevitably the meat will be impacted if the salt loses its saltiness. In other words, if the church becomes impotent as a preserving agent in the world, the 'city of man' that it is to be preserved will more rapidly begin to rot as the lifeless carcass that it is apart from Christ. If the body of Christ becomes weak, what hope is left for the building blocks that hold the world together by any measure of truth? With the decline of the intellect, so go the church and the culture. This is the present dilemma we are faced with, but it is not our only dilemma concerning the intellect.

From Augustine to Calvin to Edwards, most theologians who begin to tackle this topic of intellectualism will eventually be found coming to two conclusions. First, they will say that the intellect does hold a proper place. In the life of the human, this God-given faculty has a degree of reliability that is supposed to be stood upon when discerning the truths of the world. In the field of philosophy, the role of the intellect can always be found in the three distinct majors of epistemology, ethics, and metaphysics. Even in anthropology, the intellect has been given its own field of study known as 'Psychology', which since the early 20th century has been broken into even more specific fields dealing with cognition. Biblically, we find much mention of the mind of man, the mind of God, or the reasoning of the saints. So, we find great reason for Christian theologians throughout history to come to the conclusion that the mind plays an important role in the human. The second thing most Christian theologians say of the intellect is that although it has a proper place, this proper place can only be *a place* if it has boundaries. Therefore, the intellect is limited. Many will disagree with at least one of these views. Some will, quite wrongly, say the intellect has no place in the Christian life since it is by faith alone we are saved and live. Others, quite wrongly, will say that it is only by the faculty of the intellect we even know the object of that faith and therefore know God. Both extremes, one called fideism and the other rationalism, do not place the intellect in its true light.

It is my belief, like many of those who have walked this road before me, that the intellect has a proper place in the life of man, and specifically in the salvation and sanctification of God's people. In this place, it is neither to be neglected nor overrun, nor given more land than it was designed to occupy. To pursue either of these extremes would lead to a misshapen lens. To approach the employment of street-fighting logic from either direction starts the whole endeavor on a wrong foot. Tending toward one side or the other always creates a wholly disproportionate person. It leads to a skewed view of self, God, and the world. It would lead to the perverted intellect; the unknowing, unbelieving man.

So, what is the intellect? I used the word multiple times in the preceding paragraphs and throughout this text thus far, and I am likely to use it many more times. What is it that we are talking about? How do we define something that seems so ethereal? If we ask Freud this question, he would give us one answer that is wholly different than the one would get from Aquinas. Most philosophers would agree that the primary quality that separates man from brute animal is the rational mind. Most theologians would say that it is not only the rational mind that separates us from brute animals, but also the human spirit. However, the mind and the spirit are often seen as inseparable pairs, if not a dual unity in a reciprocating relationship within the soul. So, where do we start by defining the intellect? Let us start by going to that which should be our authority, especially on a subject like this. We will start with the Bible.

'Intellect' derives from the Latin word *intellegere* which means *to perceive*. You will not find the word 'intellect' in most modern translations of the Bible. The closest we find is the use of 'intelligence'. It is obviously closely related in its root, but shows up only a hand full of times. Its use in the Old and New Testaments often sporadic. Some translations render the same Hebrew or Greek word as 'intelligence', 'prudent', or 'understanding'. The Hebrew word often rendered as 'understanding' is תבון (tabûn). According to the B.D.B Lexicon this is a masculine noun which could mean insight, intelligence, or reason. The other use is לב (leb), which could mean inner man, heart, or conscience. The New Testament renders it 'prudent', συνετός (sunetos) in Greek. According to Strong's Dictionary this could mean 'mentally put together' or 'sagacious'.

Whichever route we take, we find a common theme that links the intellect with that of the mental and rational insight, but being something distinct from attributes like feelings or love. Based from what information we have so far, I would like to define the intellect by using both positive and negative conceptual boundaries: the intellect is the faculty of the person that consciously identifies by laws of valid inference, reasoning and logically justifying our sensory perception and extra-personal revelation to arrive at truths, but is not itself affection, faith, or wisdom. Therefore, the intellect will mainly refer to the rational or logical aspect of a person; which we will see in the bible is closely tied to, and sometimes indistinguishable from, the heart itself.

So, now that we hopefully have some idea of what we are dealing with, what is the intellect for in a Christian, and what role is it to play? In a sense, what is the goal of the intellectual capabilities, and therefore employing street-fighting logic, for the Christian life? Before we define the correct use of such a faculty and get ahead of ourselves, let us take some time to see how either the mind has been used in the past, or how it is currently being used. In the end, I hope to show that the perverted intellect, on either extreme, is no mark of a faithful Christian. The perverted intellect is the intellect that is either placed in a central location in the life of a person, or is neglected and marginalized. As Chesterton once said, "What we call the intellectual world is divided into two types of people – those who worship the intellect and those who use it. There are exceptions; but, broadly speaking, they are never the same people. Those who use the intellect never worship it; they know too much about it. Those who worship the intellect never use it; as you can see by the things they say about it." [150] John Stott, that great English preacher and evangelist, stated it thus in the first chapter of *Your Mind Matters*: "I shall issue some cautions against jumping out of the frying pan and into the fire, that is, against abandoning a superficial anti-intellectualism in favor of an arid hyper-intellectualism. I am not pleading for a dry, humorless, academic Christianity, but for a warm devotion set on fire by truth. I long for this biblical balance and the avoidance of fanatical extremes. I shall urge that the remedy for an exaggerated view of the intellect is neither to disparage it, nor neglect it, but to keep it in its God-appointed place, fulfilling its God-appointed role." [151] The intellect becomes perverted when you either exalt it to a hyper-acclaimed post or condemn it to a hyper-neglected post. In essence, it is taken out of its rightful place when either inappropriately praised or oppressed. With the intellect, the human has always done one of two things apart from using it correctly. He either impoverishes the intellect or he imprisons it.

The Impoverished Intellect

Though the battleground that holds the wars between rationalism and faith are nothing new to the ecumenical narrative of the Christian church, or philosophical journals, what began to take place in the Western world during the 18th century has produced a far grander effect on society and the local church like never before. On the hinges of piety and revival swung the massive door of what we now call anti-intellectualism, or irrationalism. It began with a deep desire to see the church expand and a sincere motivation to love the Lord with enthusiastic convictions. However, what resulted were the neglect of structure and the loss of orthodoxy. The massive door swung open, allowing emotivism and subjectivism to sweep the church floor clean of strict doctrinal adherence and conservatism. Thus, rushing through the church doors were the primary characters of Feeling and Experience who bound and kicked out the backdoor the previous Puritan occupants of Critique and Reason. Many scholars speak to this 'Great Awakening' as one of the biggest shifts in Western church culture which has brought us to our current state.

As the earlier quote from J.P. Moreland stated, the church has taken much of the backlash from this shift and has even been the instigator in many respects. We have hoards of congregations and pastors who no more theologically know what they believe and why than who know the proper structure of a Modus Ponens argument. We have youth leaders who find it more beneficial to invest efforts in building new facilities for video games and youth movies rather

implication elimination

"P implies Q; P is asserted to be true, so Q must be true"

modus ponens example:
If it is raining, I will meet you at the theater.
It is raining.
Chapter Four – The Goal   125
Therefore ~ etc

than concentrate their attention on equipping parents to teach and disciple their children in thought, word, and deed. We have Christian grade schools who are more concerned with the next football state championship rather than teaching the students about the thinking and momentum of the culture in which they are engulfed. We have confessing Christian parents who have instilled in their child that God is in the business of 'personal happiness as defined by each individual'. And, unlike A.W Tozer who said something to the effect of, "I don't speak over the heads of my congregation, I speak through the heads of my congregation because there is nothing there to stop it!", we have pastors of large mega-churches who would rather pet the heads of their flock rather than fill it with Scripture.

Again, this is not simply an ecclesial problem, though it is certainly worse that it is this. It is also an American problem. It is a remnant and product of post-modern thinking that has been allowed to run rampant through the halls of academia and streets of our most populated cities. "Live. Laugh. Love." is a popular new phrase that is often found stamped to the foreground of a cheap piece of plastic, with kitsch paintings in the background. However, no one bothers to ask, "How should we live? When should we laugh? Whom should we love?" It is left open, without direct objects to each verb, and vacant of any real substance, reflecting the quality of the modern intellect. We no longer want to exert any more energy on understanding this dilemma than it takes to hang this piece of 'art' on our wall. We simply let our hearts take us where they will and check our brains at the door, even in the places we should use them most, like universities. We are intellectually bankrupt and have suffered for it in our public squares, private prayers, and political chairs. These are the effects of the impoverished mind. Hence, there is a great need to recover a proper understanding and practice of logic.

One of the side-effects of schools no longer teaching a formal class on logic is that grown-ups don't know how to think clearly. They muddle issues, swatting at gnats while simultaneously feeding dragons. Many in our pop culture, whether celebrity or the common Joe, know some talking points they see between television commercials or on morning radio, but haven't spent much time thinking fully through the issues. There are many reasons for this. But one of the effects is that arguments end up becoming about peripheral issues, issues not central to what is at the core of the topic or the core of the disagreement. Therefore, a wise arguer will know how to discern gnats from dragons, and in so doing they will make the resolution, "I will swat at gnats when all the dragons are slain."

Practically, this means that the core issues must be dealt with first in an argument before moving on to the more insignificant ones. Bad arguers, or crafty arguers who want to avoid stating their real position on a topic, will point at the gnats all around, ensuring that the conversation goes there rather than where it should go. These are often called informal fallacies (fallacies of distraction, fallacies of ambiguity, and fallacies of form), but they are also more than that. 'Fallacious gnats' can also take the form of changing topics quickly or speaking around an issue. They can be actual distractions at a grocery store or they can be conversational or topical distractions when discussing one's political views. Chasing fallacious gnats does nothing but allow the dragons to live one more day, wreaking havoc on our interpersonal relationships, social dealings, and intellectual disciplines.

The Imprisoned Intellect   fallacies of distraction
                    "   ambiguity
          "   form

On the opposite side, we find those who elevate the intellect, sitting under it and giving themselves as its footstool. This is not the current default mode of the church as it would imply an excess of trust in the intellect. Nonetheless, intellectualism, especially at the expense of far greater gifts, is often fiercely sought after by many well-intentioned Christians. Thus, serving and enslaved to it, the Christian scholar makes it his prime identity to be defined and known by the depth and density of his mind. He finds himself consistently praising it for its wonderful works and eventually seeking to honor it with all his heart, soul, mind, and strength. Before he knows it, he finds himself a citizen on the flying island of Laputa, greeting Gulliver. Or he has become caged by his own pursuits, like the deplorable professor in John Bunyan's *Pilgrim's Progress*. Though John Bunyan intended this to be a professing believer and not an academic professor, a dose of conjecture and heap of overlay allows us to see parallels between this character's state and that of those who become imprisoned by an over-abundant reliance on the intellect.

The first question that Christian asks the caged man is simple. "What are you?" The answer the man gives is much more profound than the question warranted. He replies, "I am what I was not once." The caged man continues, "I was once a fair and flourishing Professor, both in mine own eyes, and also in the eyes of others; I once was, as I thought, fair for the Celestial City, and had then even joy at the thoughts that I should get thither." The caged man starts by disclosing his previous profession, as we would suspect of those who glory in academic titles. It is the first piece of information we learn directly from the character. Its placement in the sequence is important. So, what was this character? What do people first tell us about themselves, and therefore what does that tell us about them, really? If we read this character as an academic professor, then we could say he was a popular and progressive scholar, by both his own appraisal and the appraisal of others. He was once running hard after God and his Kingdom, by both his own appraisal and the appraisal of others. He even tells us he was excited and hyper-pious at the thought of arriving at heaven's gates. He was formerly a model for all Christians who pursue to mature their intellect.

Not only can we learn from what the professor said about himself, it is helpful to realize that which he did not say, and perhaps what most academicians would not tell us upon first meeting them and asking who they are. Again, reading the caged man in Bunyan's story as an academic professor, why did he go automatically to his vocational post? Why did he go straight to his personal and social renown? Christian asked him a very open-ended question that could have taken any direction. He could have told us about his family. He could have told us about his upbringing and nationality. He could have stated the obvious, that he was a man that was once free and is now in a cage. Yet, the Bunyan's character, like many whose idol is their intellect, chose this one direction. He was simply asked to identify himself, yet in identifying himself he revealed himself even more imprisoned. Even in his cage, he could not get away from first identifying himself with what first got him caged. His identity prior to imprisonment was that of an intellectual, a scholar. Now being caged, he is still that. He will always be that. He has become, like in the Old Testament, the idols which he worshiped. He wanted so desperately to be known as a world-renown intellectual, and obviously still does, that he eventually got his wish. He has become the intellectual he hoped to be, metal bars and all. When a rationalist becomes like his idols, he loses his heart.

The intellect, in and of itself, is not a horrific thing. God instructs us to "…love the Lord your God with all your heart and

with all your soul and with all your *mind* and with all your strength."
(Mark 12:30) It was the Christian church that faithfully started the
first universities and institutions of higher learning in the west. It
was Christian clerics who were some of the only citizens throughout
history to be literate or hold the first academic degrees. It was a
search for godly truth that began the discipline of most sciences
(material and immaterial).   So, how could someone get in the
situation of the caged professor in Bunyan's story? Or is this just an
isolated event we read into the story, with no evidence in our
everyday dealings? This is not an isolated event that is projected into
a complex allegory while being unfounded in the real world. We
must understand that both theology and the employment of the
intellect are dangerous tasks. I believe Bunyan was envisioning a
realistic situation when he decided to place this loud warning in his
famous work, and I believe we are right to conjecture that this caged
man was perhaps the best theologian around.

These two extremes, that of the impoverished intellect and that
of the imprisoned intellect, are just two more means by which man
attempts to exalt himself above God, seeking righteousness on his
own accord. These are the extremes we find when dealing with the
intellect. These are the extremes we hope to avoid, bringing us
where the intellect is properly used to save sinners and sanctify
saints.

> to seek Truth
>   + goodness
> disseminate beauty

The Intellect's Role in Salvation

If street-fighting logic is ultimately about man and the glory of
the Triune God, then it would stand to reason that it is ultimately
about the salvation of man and the maturity of the Church. Thus,
we would do well to understand the nature of the intellect in the
salvation of man. Salvation is the grace of God, through the work
(life, death, resurrection, ascension, and session) of Jesus Christ by

reconciliation
holy orders
matrimony
christian burial

the witness of the Holy Spirit, that imputes justifying righteousness to the Christian, is apprehended by God-given faith, and signally sealed by the holy sacraments of baptism and communion. In short, salvation is God's promise that we are freed from sin and its punishment. This definition rightly encompasses the primacy of the Spirit's role, the centrality of God-given grace through God-given faith, and proclaims the importance of the holy sacraments in the affirmation of saving grace.   ↳ *Jimmy Akin's book*

In affirming the intellect's role in salvation, the Book of Acts gives us a good start. "And as he was saying these things in his defense, Festus said with a loud voice, 'Paul, you are out of your mind; your great learning is driving you out of your mind.' But Paul said, 'I am not out of my mind, most excellent Festus, but I am speaking true and rational words. For the king knows about these things, and to him I speak boldly. For I am persuaded that none of these things has escaped his notice, for this has not been done in a corner. King Agrippa, do you believe the prophets? I know that you believe.' And Agrippa said to Paul, 'In a short time would you persuade me to be a Christian?' And Paul said, 'Whether short or long, I would to God that not only you but also all who hear me this day might become such as I am—except for these chains.'" (Acts 26:24-29) Many times throughout the New Testament we find the disciples in the synagogues and on the streets of the town ministering and reasoning with both learned and unlearned. Why is this? Why did they bother? Acts 26 gives us a great picture of Paul's own attempt in the presence of kings and lay-jews to rationally discuss his innocence and truth of the gospel in the hopes that many may come to the same saving grace that found him. The Greek word translated 'rational' in the passage is σωφροσύνη (sōphrosunē), which also means soundness of mind, sobriety, or sanity. Man has been so designed that sobriety of mind is to be respected. A rational mind is a mind that is, for the most part, a reliable entity to be respected and employed by all men. A madman who stumbles onto the stand in a judicial trial and provides a true account of an innocent man on death-row is much more likely to be scoffed at, though his account is true, as opposed to a man in his right mind who cunningly lies through his testimony. A rational mind is a much respected tool and a faculty to be greatly desired. In fact, at the culmination of Paul's testimony at the end of Acts chapter twenty-six, we see a private conversation between the governors, Agrippa, and Festus where they conclude that Paul is indeed innocent, or at least has "...done nothing to deserve death or imprisonment" (v31). It was Paul's actions that got him to trial to begin with, but Paul's rational words that convinced the leadership of his innocence.

For the sake of the current topic, we have to consider that Paul's appeal to reasonable argumentation is not just to prove his innocence, but to prove the truth of the Gospel (particularly, the deity of Jesus of Nazareth) so that many Jews present would hear and believe. When Agrippa explicitly asks Paul if he is trying to 'persuade' him, Agrippa uses the Greek word πείθω (peithō) which means to convince by argument while using evidence or authority. It is the same Greek word that Paul uses in Romans chapter eight, verse thirty-eight when he states, "For I am sure [persuaded, πείθω] that neither death nor life, nor angels nor rulers, nor things present nor things to come, nor powers, nor height, nor depth, nor anything else in all creation, will be able to separate us from the love of God in Christ Jesus our Lord." Even more important than the etymology of the diction, note that Paul does not refute Agrippa's claim that he is indeed trying to persuade him. In fact, Paul affirms it and even says that he is not only trying to persuade Agrippa, but everyone who is listening to his testimony.

Being convinced in one's mind of the truths of the gospel through the words of man is an important step to coming to saving knowledge in Jesus Christ. For certainly, being unconvinced in one's mind of the truths of the gospel, in spite of the reasons, is one of the most formidable detractions to coming to saving knowledge in Jesus Christ. Therefore, in the practice of street-fighting logic and evangelism, the intellect must be accounted for. Even some of our most distinguished, former theologians understood this, as has been uncovered in previous chapters. "[Jonathan] Edwards esteemed the necessity of having a 'rational brain'. He demanded that all things in the soul of man should be governed by reason, the highest faculty of our being. 'Without the capacity of rational argument, all our proof of God ceases,' he argued. Reason can be trusted to reach rationally convincing, theological conclusions..." [152]

As I mentioned before, many times throughout the New Testament we find the disciples in the synagogues and on the streets of the town ministering and reasoning with both learned and unlearned. What is ironic is most often it is the unlearned and poor who are humbled and come to salvation. The learned seem to become even more outraged which often times leads to the arrest and even death of the disciples. Why? Why does reason not work with these people? If anyone should be tweaked back to a right understanding, it should be the learned who respect the fine logic being used and therefore come to Christ because of the arguments. But again, we often times find the opposite.

We find the opposite because it is not reason which ultimately pricks the heart, but the Spirit. It was affirmed well by John Gill when he comments on King Agrippa's comments to Paul in the same passage quoted earlier from Acts. "...and indeed [Agrippa] can only be an almost Christian, that becomes one merely through the persuasion of men: it is one part of the Gospel ministry to

persuade men, but this of itself is ineffectual; a real Christian is
made so by the power of divine grace. Agrippa was only persuaded,
and but almost persuaded by the apostle to be a Christian, but not
by the Lord, nor altogether, who persuades Japheth to dwell in the
tents of Shem." And to finish Jonathans Edwards's quote in the
least section, "…Yet reason, Edwards argued, was insufficient
without revelation." [153] Calvin said it this way, "…the testimony of
the Spirit is more excellent than all reason. For as God alone is a fit
witness of himself in his Word, so also the Word will not find
acceptance in men's hearts before it is sealed by the inward
testimony of the Spirit." [154] And later in the Institutes he states,
"Since reason, therefore, by which man distinguishes between good
and evil, and by which he understands and judges is a natural gift,
it could not be completely wiped out [by original sin]; but it was
partly weakened and partly corrupted, so that its misshapen ruins
appear…First, in man's perverted and degenerate nature some
sparks still gleam. These show him to be a rational being, differing
from brute beasts, because he is endowed with understanding. Yet,
secondly, they show this light choked with dense ignorance, so that
it cannot come forth effectively." [155]

This talk of ineffectual argumentation and depraved rationality
is crucial and cannot be overlooked when discussing the topic of the
intellect's role in man's salvation. John Stott once commented, "It is
quite true that man's mind shared in the devastating results of the
Fall. The 'total depravity' of man means that every constituent part
of his humanness has been to some degree corrupted, including his
mind, which Scripture describes as 'darkened.' " [156] Second
Corinthians, chapter three, explains that it is only through a
softened mind that we may see the Lord, our minds can only be
softened by turning to Christ, and we can only turn to Christ by the
freedom which comes from the Lord who is Spirit. The veil of

unbelief is not lifted from the hardened heart until the Spirit moves upon the face of the unbeliever. Therefore, it is not the lifeless soul that sprinkles itself with reason and lifts its veil with its stammering hands as it tries to understand and capture the great truths of the Gospel. Belief is not a matter of having the proper reasons for believing or assenting to the right propositions, for good reason is used by both the sinner and the saint for very different ends. Rather, belief is a matter of trusting in the effectual work of Christ through humility and faith, not merely reason and rhetoric.

For analogy, a dirty man who attempts to clean himself off with his dirty hands does no more good for himself than spread the filth further throughout his body, causing it to penetrate even deeper into his pores. This is what is meant by the depraved intellect being insufficient to save man. On this, I will agree with St. Augustine and Martin Luther that the intellect of an unregenerate man is certainly corrupt with sin and is unstable. As Martin Luther comments on Genesis 8:21 and 6:5, "He does not say that it is 'intent on' or 'prone to' evil, but that it is wholly evil, and that nothing but evil is thought of or imagined by man throughout his life." The unregenerate heart uses reason to denounce God while many believing hearts use reason to prove him. What's the difference? Reason is being used in both scenarios in order to sway the other person, yet we so often see neither person swayed. Therefore, the difference is the unregenerate heart, the choice of God based on His own reasons.

Consider a scenario, a case-study if you will. I have been evangelizing both Robby and Marcus for the past two years. Robby is a history professor at Local University and Marcus is an electrician who lives down the street. I meet with them separately at a coffee-shop once a week and they know nothing of one another. In regards to their problems and disputes with Christian teaching, they are at the same place. Both cannot see how a God, allowing himself to be crucified, could possibly save people from this mysterious place called Hell. Let's suppose I introduce the same argument, bible verses, and rational to both of them and allow them to chew it over for a while. What is it that will bring one to belief and keep the other in unbelief? Is it that one finally sees how it all makes sense? Is it that one will go home, do a scientific and philosophical analysis on crucifixion, Hell, and the character of God and come up with an equation that will satisfy his disbelief? Is it that one will finally be able to find enough historical evidence to gratify his skeptical mind to believe that Christ died for his sins? Paul says that which we preach is a proclamation of folly. (1Cor. 1:21). It satisfies neither the earthly wisdom that the Greeks long for or the earthly sign that the Jews look for. What will save one of these men and not the other is imparted, extra-personal belief that comes from the gracious will of God through the power of the Holy Spirit, and nothing else. We may reason with someone for years and cover every human discipline known to man. Yet, if their heart is hardened with unbelief, reason will not be a strong enough rake to till the impenetrable, dehydrated soil. It needs the Water of Life. Chesterton said it this way:

"…it is not enough that the unhappy man should desire truth; he must desire health. Nothing can save him but a blind hunger for normality, like that of a beast. A man cannot think himself out of mental evil; for it is actually the organ of thought that has become diseased, ungovernable, and, as it were, independent. He can only be saved by will or faith. The moment his mere reason moves, it moves in the old circular rut…Curing a madman is not arguing with a philosopher; it is casting out a devil. And however quietly doctors and psychologists may go to work in the matter, their attitude is profoundly intolerant – as intolerant as Bloody Mary. Their attitude is really this: that the man must stop thinking, if he is to go on living. Their counsel is one of intellectual amputation. If thy *head* offend thee, cut it off; for it is better, not merely to enter the Kingdom of Heaven as a child, but to enter it as an imbecile, rather than with your whole intellect to be cast into hell – or into Hanwell. Such is the madman of experience; he is commonly a reasoner, frequently a successful reasoner. Doubtless he could be vanquished in mere reason, and the case against him put logically. But it can be put much more precisely in more general and even aesthetic terms." [157]

Luther's words are again helpful. "But let us hear Paul interpret himself. In the third chapter [of Romans], by way of peroration he says: 'What then? Are we better than they? In no wise; for we have proved both Jews and Gentiles to be all under sin' (v. 9). Where is 'free will' now?...You cannot find a way out by saying: though they are under sin, yet the best part in them, that is, reason and will, makes endeavours towards good. For if the endeavour that remains to them is good, Paul's statement that they are under sin is false...But wrath is revealed from heaven against them, and unless they are justified by the Spirit it will damn them, whole and entire; which would not be, were they not under sin, whole and entire!"

A bit further, consider this. What is to happen to the salvation of a human who has suffered extensive brain-damage? What is to happen to someone who is mentally retarded or cognitively handicapped? How are they to attain a saving knowledge of God if their mental faculties are damaged? This is where the true beauty of God's grace and efficacious gospel shines. First, let us be clear that God can speak into the hearts of man through any method he so chooses in order to enlighten their soul and bring them to himself. With this scenario, we must distinguish between what Jonathan Edwards calls 'speculative knowledge' and 'spiritual knowledge'.

Speculative knowledge is that which every natural man has and works hard to use in order to discern truth. He works so hard using it in every discipline that he even attempts to locate God with it. It is like using a tree-branch to detect a metal pirate ship buried far beneath a beach. However, this is all they have as they search for truth and discern the meaning of life. *Spiritual knowledge* is that special sense which is imparted to the regenerated soul. It is a proper understanding of God, self, and the new grace-enveloped relationship between the two through the ministry of the Holy Spirit. The difference between these two kinds of knowledge is as the chart below suggests:[158]

Speculative Knowledge	Spiritual Knowledge
- Comes to the natural man	- Comes to the Saint
- Depends on natural senses	- Depends on supernatural senses
- Theorizes the sensible	- Consists in a sense of heart for
- Experiences only a dead letter,	spiritual beauty
dry, lifeless, and tasteless	- Enables one to savor the
- Textual understanding of the	sufficiency of Jesus Christ as
Bible leading to factual	mediator
apprehension	- Spiritual understanding of the
- Speculates and concludes	Bible leading to obedience
inadequately by rationale	- Produces holy discernment
- Has a depraved appetite that	without logical reasoning
leads to worldly wisdom	- Has a spiritual taste that leads to
- Seeks inward suggestions and	Godly wisdom
enthusiastic facts for divine	
sensing	

	- Has a harmony between the disposition of the soul and God's word

"So spiritual disposition and godly taste teach and guide a man in his behavior in the world. An uneducated person who is deeply humble, meek, and has a loving disposition will be able to live according to Christian rules of humility, meekness, and charity far more readily and specifically than someone who does not have the disposition but studies diligently and reasons elaborately with a strong intellect." [159] Because of man's depravity, Edwards recognized that reason itself, competent as it may be, is drawn into the complicity of a corrupt human nature. Unaided, human reason cannot be expected to eradicate sin, or to accept its own limitations. Human nature's futility is in self-love infesting our reason, our conscience, and our world. So the mind is also fallen, crippled by sin. Man therefore needs more than good intentions. He needs the power of the Holy Spirit to reveal God's Word to his mind and to influence his affections.

Our minds, like our wills, cannot long for the good without the Holy Spirit. This longing does not come from our nature like the ability to reason, but from regeneration. As Calvin writes, "In this ruin of mankind no one now experiences God either as Father or as Author of salvation, or favorable in any way, until Christ as Mediator comes forward to reconcile him to us." [160]

I will end this section with a personal story. My wife and I were once a part of a congregation where every Sunday morning we would arrive and immediately begin looking for two open seats. Each week, we were pleased to look for, and settle in the row behind, one particular little girl. We did this really for one main reason: encouragement and bits of laughter. At the end of each service, the same routine occurred. The little girl stood on her chair, lifted her hands in the air, and began loudly singing with the rest of the congregation the great Doxology by Luther. "Praise God from whom all blessings flow. Praise Him all creatures here below. Praise him above ye heavenly hosts. Praise Father, Son, and Holy Ghost." Does she even know what she is singing? Does she understand the words which she sings so loudly? To this I would answer both yes and no. It depends on what we mean by 'know' or 'understand'. If by saying 'understand' we mean she has a cognitive ability to logically deduce the sermon text or hymn and place its parts in a systematic theology, I would answer she did not understand it in this way. On other occasions when we sang the *Gloria Patri*, I should not go to her, ask her to recite the whole thing, and then have her explain the Trinity and its effects on her as she sang the song. However, if by saying 'understand' we mean a God-honoring response to the Lord's service wrought by Holy Spirit, I would answer she did understand it in this way. And this childlike faith is what God calls every believer to. Childlike faith is not just a lively part of the street-fighting logician's task, it is the essential groundwork for coming to hold a position on any subject whatsoever. —— *amen* ——

Coming to Christ is ultimately not an ascent to rational propositions, having enough right answers in a row so as to explain deep and mysterious truths, even to the point of realizing they are a mystery. Coming to Christ is ultimately a Spirit driven, humble, inquisitive, meek, eager, and lively response to the glorious Gospel. It is an understanding of, or a 'standing under', truth. This is one of the reasons why children are so important to keep close to the life of the Church, though it is not hard to find a church in every city that herds them into a nursery room or Sunday school class so to avoid disturbing the 'grown-up' worship service. Not only does

doesn't sound like a pre-destinationist

Scripture commend children to be a part of the Church, their presence is a reminder of a great reality. We need to bring our children back into our fold for every interaction, especially Sunday mornings. Often times, they 'get it' much more than many of the church's lifelong members. Surely, this is one of the reasons why in the tenth chapter of Mark's gospel and the eighteenth chapter of Luke's gospel Jesus rebuked his disciples and said, "Let the children come to me; do not hinder them, for to such belongs the kingdom of God. Truly, I say to you, whoever does not receive the kingdom of God like a child shall not enter it." Children are signs of life. Their vibrancy and vitality are bursting from them and they cannot help relinquishing it into the world. In the heart of a young person redeemed by Christ, their understanding is being saturated with great truths even though they may not be able to expound on them or give a rational argument for them. For the little girl who sat in front of us each Lord's day, her saving faith was of the Holy Spirit – a poetic, imaginative, and inspired faith—and not of the pure intellect. So too should be ours on subjects great and small. As Poythress put it, "Argument has an important role not only in human communication but in God's own speech to us through agents like the apostles Peter and Paul. God himself uses arguments in religious persuasion. But God is also present through the Holy Spirit to bring about inward readiness in a person's heart, and to bring subjective conviction in response to arguments and other explanations of the truth. Until God changes people's hearts, they resist the truth of the gospel." [161]

The Intellect's Role in Sanctification

Sanctification is the lifelong work of God in the life of a Christian, through the Holy Spirit and by the work (life, death, resurrection, ascension, and session) of Jesus Christ, that produces good works by faith. This comes to fruition at loving God with one's whole heart, soul, mind, and strength, and loving one's neighbor as one's self. In short, while salvation is God's promise that we are freed from sin and its punishment, sanctification is God's promise that we are freed to righteousness and its blessings. This definition encompasses growth in holiness, implies the mortification of sin, and culminates in the glory of God. This will be our working definition throughout this section.

Affirming the intellect's role in sanctification, Paul in Romans offers good insight. "I appeal to you therefore, brothers, by the mercies of God, to present your bodies as a living sacrifice, holy and acceptable to God, which is your spiritual worship. Do not be conformed to this world, but be transformed by the renewal of your mind, that by testing you may discern what is the will of God, what is good and acceptable and perfect. For by the grace given to me I say to everyone among you not to think of himself more highly than he ought to think, but to think with sober judgment, each according to the measure of faith that God has assigned." (Rom. 12:1-3) As previously stated, sanctification is first and foremost the work of God through the Holy Spirit. All things redeemed are ultimately redeemed this way and no other. In the believer, the Spirit has been deployed over the personhood of man to enact disciplines which would renew and reflect a life of holy godliness in thought, word, and deed. This is the joyous road the born-again Christian is placed upon at the point of salvation. This road, however, is not a conveyer-belt for broken, passive toys in God's factory, toys waiting to be renovated. On this road, the Lord has graciously quickened us, gifting to us many tools in order to fulfill His work and His bride. In short, He has given man responsibilities. Among these, we find the sacraments, the gathering of the church, the reading of the Word, the preaching of the Word, the daily prayers of the saints, and boldly evangelizing the lost world. Within each of these, we find the faculties of man and a will that is never neutral, but constantly inclined to either serve God or serve sin. We are given great personal disciplines to encourage the former and suffocate the latter.

So, what responsibility do we have toward our own and other's sanctification? What tools has God given us? In short, how should the intellect in the practice of street-fighting logic give itself for the present endeavor? As J.P. Moreland states, "To be sure, Christians must rely on the Holy Spirit in their intellectual pursuits, but this does not mean they should expend no mental sweat of their own defending the faith." [162]

Sanctification by intellectual sharpening does not mean simply getting smarter, though knowledge and understanding are surely part of the fruition. Sanctification by intellectual sharpening does not mean going to church more, though a desire to live and worship in community will certainly be an effect of the Gospel. Sanctification by intellectual sharpening does not mean becoming nicer, though grace and care will surely flow from a proper understanding of the grace of God. As Augustine would say of Romans 12:2, this exhortation to renew the mind is pointing to a sort of imitation. It is a corporeal imagination that takes place as the image of man is changed into the likeness of God. It is a cleansing of the "mind's eye". The mind is being purified by the renewing wisdom and knowledge that is imparted by the Holy Spirit, and responsibly maintained by His consistent grace to and through us. We therefore look upon the disciplines and characters of the world around us as wholly different endeavors and beings to be used for the glorification of God, the joy of man, and spread of the Gospel message; we are no longer enslaved to employing them for the innumerable lusts of our carnal sin. The renewing of our intellect

received

brings us to greater truth that we may walk uprightly, and thus honor God in our bodies as we are 'being transformed into the same image from one degree of glory to another.' (2 Cor. 3:18)

The passage stated at the start of this section from Romans is one of the most well-known passages regarding the mind's role within Christian sanctification. Verse two stands out above the rest. "Do not be conformed to this world, but be transformed by the renewal of your mind, that by testing you may discern what is the will of God, what is good and acceptable and perfect." The Greek word here for 'mind' is νοῦς (nous) which also translates as intellect or understanding. It is the same root that is used throughout epistemology when speaking of 'noetic structures'. The Greek word for 'transform' is μεταμορφόω (metamorphoō) and can also be translated as a change or transfiguring. According to this verse, the health and vitality of the intellect is at the very center of holy discernment, and consequently the center of presenting your body as a living sacrifice to God. The chain of command in these few verses is not difficult to follow.

A renewed mind deters
↳ *conforming to the world*, which ushers in
  ↳ *holy discernment* that allows us to
    ↳ *present our bodies as a living sacrifice* so that we can
      ↳ *fulfill our spiritual worship* to God.

A renewed mind is inevitably how we fulfill our spiritual worship to God. Consequently, an unrenewed mind is how we do not fulfill our spiritual worship to God. So, what is wrong with our Christian cultures and categories of thinking? In neglecting our minds, we have neglected a proper spiritual worship. If truth is what edifies the mind and sets us free, and reason can help to bring us to a better understanding of truth, then reason can be a great tool we use to edify our minds away from the deceit and dishonesty of a world that is more of a mirage than an actual waterhole.

For more fortification on the subject, the New Testament presents us with still more verses on the parallels between the mind and vitality, or demise, of the human soul: Matthew 16:23, Romans 1:28, Romans, 8:5-7, 1 Corinthians 14:14-16, 1 Corinthians 14:19-20, 2 Corinthians 5:13-15, 2 Timothy 3:6-8, and Philippians 1:6-11.

Again, reiterating what was stated in Romans 12:1-3, we come to Ephesians 4:17-25. "Now this I say and testify in the Lord, that you must no longer walk as the Gentiles do, in the futility of their minds. They are darkened in their understanding, alienated from the life of God because of the ignorance that is in them, due to their hardness of heart. They have become callous and have given themselves up to sensuality, greedy to practice every kind of impurity. But that is not the way you learned Christ!—assuming that you have heard about him and were taught in him, as the truth is in Jesus, to put off your old self, which belongs to your former manner of life and is corrupt through deceitful desires, and to be renewed in the spirit of your minds, and to put on the new self, created after the likeness of God in true righteousness and holiness. Therefore, having put away falsehood, let each one of you speak the truth with his neighbor, for we are members one of another." 'Mind' in this verse is the same Greek word *nous*. What we find unique in these verses is that the vitality and direction of the mind is no longer strictly a vertical affair in which only my relationship with God is affected. It is also a horizontal one in which my relationship with my neighbor is affected. Putting on the new self, which is part of doing away with falsehood, envy, and malice, is the initiator which allows me to appropriately speak truth with my neighbor.

We cannot mature in love of God + neighbor
with out the transformed mind.

Chapter Four — The Goal   145

The metamorphosis of the intellect is at the center of the two greatest commands to love our God and love our neighbor. Certainly we cannot mature unless we are maturing in these two privileging responsibilities, and certainly we cannot mature in these two privileging responsibilities unless we are cultivating a Christian mind, through and through.

Though we have certainly concluded the intellect's very special role in the sanctification of a Christian, we must now ask ourselves if it is to hold an ultimate role. It is safe to say that the man who dares to come before God after the last trump, reasoning his way into belief and glory, finds himself enraptured in a tangle of babble. His response should be praise and his end should be worship. The man who dares to sanctify himself by flawlessly reasoning why he should and should not do something will only find his feeble heart inclined to do evil. His justifying arguments will quickly turn against him. Only a love for God and love for neighbor, instilled and matured by the Holy Spirit upon the merits of Christ, will be the final avenue to holiness. Upon this, our end could never be self-praise or adoration for our pure logic and strong intellect. In other words, rationalism cannot sanctify.

As Paul in Philippians tells us, "And the peace of God, which surpasses all understanding, will guard your hearts and your minds in Christ Jesus." (Phil. 4:7) Before we break these down further, let us notice for a bit what the verse does not say. It does not say, "And the reason of man, which surpasses all ignorance, will guard your hearts and your minds in Christ Jesus." It does not say, "And the logical arguments, which surpasses all unbelief, will guard your hearts and your minds in Christ Jesus." It does not say, "And the intellect of man, which surpasses all faculties, will guard your belief in Christ Jesus." It is important to note that the Greek word for 'understanding' in this verse is the same word we have followed thus far. It is νοῦς (nous), which like earlier forms translates as intellect or understanding. And the Greek word for 'minds' is νόημα (noēma) translates as perception, purpose, or intellect.

Throughout the life and maturation of a Christian, one's intellect may be satisfied, the logical arguments considered and found complete. Still, his heart may remain in despair until holiness comes to dwell through the peace of God. All are insecure and restless to some degree until they at last behold the face of God with an unveiled face. And as long as we are on this side of heaven, we will see with veiled faces. Therefore, it is only the peace of God, which 'surpasses' (ὑπερέχω/huperechō: is superior to, excels, is better than) the mind of man that can ensure we remain in Christ Jesus. And remaining in Christ Jesus is the only way to be sanctified. The context of the Philippians verse stated above is important to note. It comes near the end of the epistle and is surrounded by verses where Paul speaks directly in 'sanctification' jargon. Start in chapter three, verse twelve. It begins with the persistence with which we should run the race, understanding that we are not yet perfect. A little further we find Paul encouraging the reader to imitate him and walk in accordance with his leadership, which would be one of faithfulness and maturation. And after the above stated verse we find a list of virtues which should characterize our thought, and therefore our lives: 'just', 'true', 'honorable', 'lovely' 'commendable', 'excellence', 'practice' (πράσσω/prassō: habitually perform).

The completed effect of sanctification is a growing knowledge and love for God. This is undeniably scattered throughout the Scriptures. Those who are truly being sanctified can only do so by knowing and loving God, and loving God is always one of the two primary results of sanctification. The other is love for neighbor. Even after our conversion, as we seek to dwell in the house of the Lord, hide his word in our hearts, and glorify Him in our bodies, reason maintains its limitations. If we are right in saying that growing in knowledge and love of God is not just an effect, but also a means by which we are sanctified, then surely the more we do grow in our knowledge of God the more we are being sanctified. However, reason itself has great limitations when attempting to know and love God in this way.

All who have studied the character of God and His attributes know that the most formidable doctrine a Christian will ever encounter is the doctrine of the Trinity. For millennia now, scholars, philosophers, and theologians have racked their heads and wore away their fingertips hoping to express this mysterious reality. They have searched the manuscripts and creeds in hopes of adding their stroke to the history of all those who have attempted to take on the difficult task of exposing this glorious reality: God is both three and one. This topic is often the culmination of many theological works. After years of ministry and service, it just so happens that most saintly intellectuals finally gain enough courage to attempt their hand at the cards. This is no coincidence. The Trinity is undoubtedly the most distinguished doctrine in the Christian faith. It is the primary doctrine which separates Christians from Pantheist, Muslims, and Buddhists. It is at the center of the controversies which caused most heretics to be labeled as such. A study of the Trinity is an investigation into the Godhead's interrelatedness and self-sufficiency as Three in One. Proper reason and tight logic are always two of the most useful tools when attempting to understand and teach this doctrine. However, the intellect falls short in its ability to truly sanctify our souls by a perfect glimpse of God as three in one.

By nearly any man's measure, Saint Thomas Aquinas has been one of the leading proponents of the intellects role in Christian faith. Reason, often by way of the scholastic method, is scattered throughout his work, both major and minor treatises. From writing about the Trinity to expounding a Christian aesthetics, Aquinas never ceases to cite reason's role. And when he does so, it is seldom a passing thought. For Aquinas, the intellect is used as a substantive ingredient to understanding the topic at hand. For him it is necessary and natural that reason acts as one of the key functions of the human when grappling with any subject at whatever depth. However, even he conceded that reason can only get us so far in our attempt to fully know, and therefore rest in, the Triune God. As he states, "That God is three and one is only known by belief, and it is in no way possible for this to be demonstratively proven by reason, however much to this end some sort of reasons are given, they are neither necessary nor even very likely unless the articles of faith are already held...the Trinity of Persons is not able to be perceived by means of reasoning from divine causality itself, because divine causality is common to the total Trinity. Nor can a reasoning of a Trinity of Persons be accomplished by means of remotion. Hence it is in no way possible for reason to demonstratively prove that God is three and one." [163]

St. Thomas Aquinas understood the limits of human reason, even in times of his most potent advocacy of it. Accurately knowing God, and therefore being truly sanctified, is never accomplished by mere reason, but by a reasonable faith. Reason alone cannot pull us out of the sticky cobweb of sin that so easily entangles us. It cannot quicken our lifeless corpse as it lay dead in the cobweb of sin, and it cannot lift our hands from the threads of that cobweb in order to mortify and repent from dabbling in that cobweb ever again. Our souls are made alive and purified through the power of the Holy Spirit by the grace of God. Even a redeemed intellect must, at some point, realize in itself its own inadequacies, therefore humbly submitting to a faith that is lovingly imparted from outside its own reach.

The Faithful Intellect

So, what can we conclude of the intellect? The dead soul cannot be brought to life by anything other than the breath of the Spirit. And the quickened soul cannot be matured into glory by any other principle than that of the Holy Spirit. If anything, the Spirit may use reason to bring the dead, dismembered-by-sin body closer to the surface from the cold depths of sin's deep ocean. But, even then, you still only have a lifeless, disintegrated corpse, not as deep as it once was and still submerged in vast nothingness; and therefore a lifeless corpse that has been nothing more than relocated. Even this metaphor may not fully capture the proper role of reason. It will ultimately be a Spirit-wrought faith which will sanctify our souls and cast our anxiety upon the redeeming hand of our Maker.

How are we to see our intellect? How can we avoid perverting it by either impoverishing it or imprisoning it? And what can we employ in order to ensure an adequate balance of use, without a disproportionate reliance or naïve neglect? As Douglas Hall states, "As reason extends itself to its limits, that which was previously by faith is no longer always of faith, but is known naturally. Such can be the case with revealed truths which include naturally knowable truths. But in the dominion of faith, reason will ultimately come face-to-face with its limits to understanding, and it is at these limit-points that reason is to open itself before the mystery rather than undertaking judgment which would render the infinite mystery a finity, comprehensible, objective "fact"…it is a divine gift of wisdom which enables the faith-filled person to live in this tension of faith and reason." [164]

This quote comes right in the middle of Hall's exposition of Aquinas's understanding of the Trinity. It seems that what the Christian faith calls us to when it speaks of understanding is something altogether different from Aristotle's pursuit of metaphysics. When studying the fanciful logic of the Greeks and the eloquent oratories of the Romans, we should do so while remaining outside a blanket of concentration and complete admiration, for it is certain that our sinful hearts will yearn to become like them. Consequently, while idolizing past intellects, we will rely on our own ability to reason and rationally justify ourselves in and out of even the most holy of biblical categories, all the while perverting scripture and enrapturing ourselves in a cold, metal cage of precise argumentation and self-justification.

We ought to believe with Augustine that the mind is both an active and a passive agent. It is active in that we utilize it to judge and relate sense experiences to something besides the precise experience itself. It is passive in that even the mind itself did not derive from itself, but from a greater being which provided being to it; just as the moon derives its light it reflects from the sun. However, we cannot go so far as W.T. Stace and say that all logic must be banned from religion. As Ronald Nash states, "Once logic is denied, inconsistency becomes a virtue." [165] And I do not stand in the Amsterdam Philosophy of Dooyeweerd whose implications of his Boundary system on the whole of human knowledge seem to, as Plantinga states, "...end in gnosticism and incoherence." [166] Dooyeweerd's system crumbles with one simple question, "Will there be reasoning in heaven, when we are finally with the Lord, on his side of the Boundary?" There is great support (logical, empirical, or revelatory) that can be found on 'this side of the Boundary' to believe so, and that God would have it no other way so that his creation may come to know him on 'either side of the Boundary'.

→ Making it (truth) up as you go along –
Christian

As Christians, and therefore thinkers, we must repudiate the double theory of truth found in men like Siger of Brabant and Paul Tillich. And we are right to side with Aristotle's view on the law of non-contradiction, in that it is a law of thought because it is first a law of being. It is a law rooted in all of reality and therefore is a basic belief which needs no inference or prior argument. As many have seen fit to proclaim, reason is not something that binds God and constrains him, it is more of an attribute of God, though not an attribute like holiness or goodness. "[And the affects of] sin may hinder the ability to reason correctly but it does not alter the laws of valid inference." [167] Therefore, we as Christians should be greatly concerned with the branches of philosophy (epistemology, metaphysics, and ethics). We should, however, not make this our primary concern as to place it in a position as our savior. The faithful Christian needs a kind of truth which exceeds his own rational capacities. This is not to say it would be an irrational thing to accept a truth that he cannot himself grasp, but receives first. What we need is reason that is compatible with human condition. We need an expansion of the understanding of reason that will involve an acceptance of authority as not something merely to be later substituted as mere opinion, but an acceptance of an authority as something with a dignity and a reverence, which involves elements of trust. In this way, as was said earlier, truth is personal and interpersonal. Understanding reason this way would, at a fundamental level, defeat the pride of life.

What the reasonable, Christian faith calls us to is a saturation of graceful wisdom. What we need is a wise and certainly reasonable faith. Of course, there are ways to cultivate and pave the way for adequate inspiration. However, I shall say along with Patrick Sherry that inspiration is ultimately a wholly gratuitous happening that can neither be predicted through sequential manipulation nor controlled through systematic methodology of philosophy and argumentation. Therefore, let the dialectic have its place, yet keep the dialectic in its place.

In order to avoid the impoverishment of our intellect, and therefore avoid improperly worshiping God, let us learn to use our minds in all of life. Let us learn to use the God-given faculty of the intellect to deconstruct fallacious syllogisms by the opponents of our faith. Let us have foundational practices in our homes that are reasonable and appropriate. Let us have church disciplines that are sound and faithful. Let us kindly argue in the public square with a sober mind. Let us seek to love God with our minds, and not just whimsical emotions which are flighty and weightless, or simply pragmatic. As Francis Schaeffer states in *Escape From Reason*, "Neither conversion (the beginning of a Christian Life) nor spirituality (the growth) should be such a leap. Both are firmly related to the God who is there and the knowledge he has given us – and both involve the whole man." [168]

Christian academic and ecclesial institutions must recover disciplines like apologetics, rhetoric, and logic. We must have conversations where we are discussing how to live Christianly in our vocations. We must rid ourselves of intellectual apathy, thus prioritizing our academic acuteness over our athletic prowess. We must recover the ability to critically think and analyze both ourselves and the world around us. We must practice healthy discourse at an early age, and we must learn to baptize our minds in the Holy Trinity, not just our skin. We must learn to evangelize the minds of men and not just their emotions, so that their souls would be saturated with truth. The Lord is over all, and unless we learn to think that way we will not live that way, therefore rendering our service wholly incomplete and unfaithful.

On the opposite side of the spectrum, in order to avoid the imprisoning of the intellect, and therefore not properly worshipping God, let us foremost hope in Jesus Christ crucified, buried, raised, and ascended, and not metaphysics actualized, in order to save sinners and strengthen saints. Let us not use reason as the supreme satisfaction of our faith or our Christian service. Let us heed the words of the apostle Paul when he states, "For Christ did not send me to baptize but to preach the gospel, and not with words of eloquent wisdom, lest the cross of Christ be emptied of its power. For the word of the cross is folly to those who are perishing, but to us who are being saved it is the power of God. For it is written, 'I will destroy the wisdom of the wise, and the discernment of the discerning I will thwart.' Where is the one who is wise? Where is the scribe? Where is the debater of this age? Has not God made foolish the wisdom of the world? For since, in the wisdom of God, the world did not know God through wisdom, it pleased God through the folly of what we preach to save those who believe. For Jews demand signs and Greeks seek wisdom, but we preach Christ crucified, a stumbling block to Jews and folly to Gentiles, but to those who are called, both Jews and Greeks, Christ the power of God and the wisdom of God." (1 Cor. 1:17-24)

Christian academic and ecclesial institutions must recover disciplines like fasting, prayer, Scripture meditation, and singing. We must recover the ability to love our neighbors with our hands and dwell among the weak and poor. We must be willing to disrobe from our academic garments and minor philosophical squabbles so that the world, through our practice of unselfish love, can see a personal gospel and not merely a theoretical one, no matter how doctrinally sound it may be.

Let us utilize the intellect in all its grandness and limitation to love God and our neighbor, as has been instructed. Though many are not called to the post of an academic or scholar, it is every Christian's duty to love God with their minds. It is every Christian's privilege to be ready both in season and out of season to give a defense for their faith. It is every Christian's duty to speak truth in the place of lies. It is every Christian's duty to use well a gift of God, namely reason, as if they are putting on display love or gentleness. It is every Christian's duty to devise joyful ways in which we may more cleverly submit the disciplines of humanity under the Lordship of the Triune God.

Your Highest Rhetoric —LOVE

So for Christians who rightly employ logic, who place argumentation in its balanced place, what is our greatest proof? *Your love is your highest rhetoric.* As Christians we are not marked by rationalism but grace. We are not primarily marked by our ability to present good arguments, but our ability to live faithfully according to the decrees and commands of the one, true God. And just like rationalism has a certain stench, so does grace. As the Gorilla Poets sang, "Grace hurts harder." Grace has a certain smell. It has a certain meal-time culture. It speaks to its neighbor in a certain way. It carries a certain posture in classroom discussion. It speaks with a strategy that is not deceitful. It is a strategy which is most loving, most self-sacrificial, most substitutionary. I have often found it difficult to adhere to the rhetoric and reason of a good professor or pastor whom I see not loving his wife and family as he ought. Thus, my own appraisal of a faithful man, and thus a man from whom I should seek true wisdom, is not upon his ability to construct a perfect argument or exegete a passage from literature. My final appraisal on how learned of a man he is and how endowed with wisdom he may be is based upon how well he loves.

Classical rhetoric calls this *ethos*. As Aristotle says in his *Rhetoric*, "...the speaker must not only see that the speech shall prove its point, or persuade, but must also develop a certain character in himself and in the judge, as it matters much for persuasiveness—most of all in debate, but secondarily in lawsuits too—that the speaker should appear a certain sort of person, and that the judges should conceive him to be disposed towards them in a certain way..." [169]Aristotle goes on to say, "The speakers themselves are made trustworthy by three things; for there are three things, besides demonstrations, which made us believe. These are, intelligence, virtue and good-will...the man who is thought to have all the three qualities must win the belief of the hearers." [170] *Ethos* aids either the fortification or the destruction of a speaker's trustworthiness. To catch a fuller picture, Isocrates in his *Antidosis* is worth quoting at length:

> "...the man who wishes to persuade people will not be negligent as to the matter of character; no, on the contrary, he will apply himself above all to establish a most honourable name among his fellow-citizens; for who does not know that words carry greater conviction when spoken by men of good repute then when spoken by men who live under a cloud, and that the argument which is made by a man's life is of more weight than that which is furnished by words? Therefore, the stronger a man's desire to persuade his hearers, the more zealously will he strive to be honourable and to have the esteem of his fellow-citizens...an honourable reputation not only lends greater persuasiveness to the words of the man who possess it, but adds greater lustre to his deeds, and is, therefore, more zealously to be sought after by men of intelligence than anything else in the world." [171]

We should seek to learn from those who love truth, unapologetically. We should seek to be a lover and defender of the truth, and thus learn from those who do the same. In this way, we as Christians should love our neighbor as ourselves, seeking to free our neighbor from the falsehoods of every kind which abound on every corner, and so prove ourselves a disciple of Jesus Christ. For Christ did not say, "A new commandment I give to you, that you argue with one another: just as I have argued with you, you also are to argue with one another. By this all people will know that you are my disciples, if you argue with one another. " Neither did he say, "A new commandment I give to you, that you provide formal proofs for one another: just as I have provided formal proofs for you, you also are to provide formal proofs to one another. By this all people will know that you are my disciples, if you provide formal proofs for one another." Likewise, we do not find, "A new commandment I give to you, that you exceed one another in intelligence: just as I have exceed you in intelligence, you also are to exceed one another in intelligence. By this all people will know that you are my disciples, if you exceed one another in intelligence. " This could go on. The picture ought to be clear. We find in John 13:34, "A new commandment I give to you, that you love one another: just as I have loved you, you also are to love one another. By this all people will know that you are my disciples, if you have love for one another." While sound arguments and fine rhetoric should certainly be a part of Christians loving their neighbors, the converse is not necessarily true. Loving one's neighbor need not always include sound arguments and fine rhetoric.

Yet, in order to employ logic correctly in a given context, our observations, previous knowledge, and intuition must grant a broader knowledge of the present need. In order to love properly, we need to be able to see that sometimes an argument is not what is needed, but a kind of healing. That is to say, sometimes people are not in a place within the story of their life where they need more, tighter, or stronger arguments. They are at a place where they need Jesus Christ; a real-life experience with a Good News which can be seen, felt, smelt, heard, and tasted. And that is precisely the privilege and commission of the Church, Christ's bride. We are called to love in practical ways. That is part of the brilliance of sharing meals with people. Christ did it often. This is also where we hearken back to story, singing, and silence.

After a disagreement or quarrel, my wife and I ask each other two questions: Is it well? Can you sing to me? The first question seems to make sense for finding resolution in an argument. It is a dialectical question. Is it well? Is it well with us? Are you well with me? Is it well with our souls, our marriage, our trust and our love? Is it well with our friendship? Is it well with whoever needed to say "I'm sorry" in this situation and whoever needed to say "I forgive you"? The first question is obviously the kind to ask after conflict. But, what about the second? Can you sing to me? What does singing have to do with conflict? Well, it has a lot to do with conflict, but it has more to do with healing. As was alluded to earlier, singing as a defense for the Christian faith, and an act of love and communion, is important. Use all the tactics God has given you to love your neighbor as yourself. Use food. Use song. Use the Sacraments of the church. Use science...good science. Use art...good art. Use literature...yes, good literature. Use every sound argument and bit of God's spoken world to exude the fragrance of the Way, the Truth, and the Light. All of these are not add-ons or contradictory to the intellect. They are a kind of non-dialectic proof in themselves. They are practical and poetic ways we can love our neighbor as incarnate beings. And in so loving this way, we become new men and encourage others to follow suit.

Stay Stupid (Humble)

When we learn, we are put in community, perhaps a different community than where we were before. Each new subject, each new lesson, and each new skill acquaints us with our fellow man, the world, and God in a way that was not there in our former ignorance. The more we know, the more we can engage in conversations with peers on the same subject. And the more we know, the more we can know. This means that the more we know, the more we are able to interact on a broader scale and at a higher quality of conversation. After becoming well-educated, one might be found among the cultural elite, discussing high art and global problems. When this happens, we have a tendency to leave our former ignorance behind, which is not wholly bad, and move to more success-filled realms. In a sense, this is called maturity. In another sense, knowledge puffs up, and, as it turns out, not all cocktail parties are worth going to, and not all global-problem solvers really understand the globe, its problems, or how to solve them. Because of this, we are not to avoid learning. We are to avoid pride. And the best way to do that is to be humbled by staying stupid.

But what does it mean to stay stupid? It does not mean to be weak readers, slow thinkers, poor listeners, mumbled speakers, or incompetent writers. It likewise does not mean we trade in our books for white collars, or our white collars for blue collars, or our blue collars for overalls, or our overalls for rags. To stay stupid means to stay common, to maintain a humble humanity that is able to learn just as much from the elderly, eighth-grade-educated grocer as we can from the triple-doctorate, Nobel-Prize winner. To stay stupid means to visit family reunions while not sitting on the sidelines as you watch the hometown grubs live out their sad existence. Staying stupid means dirty hands and soft hearts. It means broad appeal and fair chance. It means engaging the local farmer on his own terms and not on yours. It means loving common sense above academia. It means discussing your grandmother's back pain without recourse to turning the conversation to your academic accomplishments. It means meeting a spouse's colleague and asking about their life without looking for a bridge to telling about your own academic degrees or latest academic project. For the Christian, staying stupid means loving others first.

Western history has had much to say about staying stupid, in the good sense. As said earlier, one must constantly recognize the limits of one's knowledge, the depth of ignorance we have, even on the subjects we know the most about. Aristotle in his *Rhetoric* discussed this in light of persuasion and listener appeal. "This is the reason why the uneducated are more persuasive than the educated for popular audiences – as the poets say of the uneducated, that 'they have a finer charm for the ear of the crowd'. Educated men state general principles and draw general conclusions; uneducated men draw conclusions, which lie close at hand, from facts within their own experience." [172] That is to say, educated men rely too heavily on deductive arguments, presenting themselves as wooden and unapproachable, two-dimensional even. They take Tozer's approach to the extreme: they don't talk over their listener's head; they only talk through it, either because there is nothing in the listener's head to capture the thought or there is just enough to capture the thought and the speaker has been quite unkind in speaking in such a way so that the listener cannot capture what is said. Hence, educated men often care more for themselves and their academic topics than for their listeners. By contrast, uneducated men have simple experience, or inductive reasoning, to draw from,

[handwritten margin note: ? what that ?]

[handwritten note at bottom: Tozer Not referenced anywhere]

so they lean there, seemingly more approachable, lifelike, and convincing than some of the greatest academicians among us. Aristotle here is not advising us to avoid deductive reasoning. He is encouraging us to stay stupid; stay common. Dr. Peter Leithart of Theopolis Institute says something similar in his 2008 commencement address to New Saint Andrews graduates titled "The Dangers of Theology": "The greatest danger is for those of you who are called to spend your lives studying and teaching theology. But whatever you plan to do with your graduate degree in theology, your training will tempt you to become a Pharisee. When some superstitious old woman gently reminds you of some basic truth of the gospel, you will be tempted to object, 'Yes, but the Greek says.' When an untrained nobody in the church wants to teach you something, you will be tempted to respond Pharisaically, as the Pharisees in fact did to the blind man, 'You want to teach us?' If he persists you will be relieved he is not part of your little club. The answer to this temptation is worship. Jesus repeatedly contrasts the honor that comes from God with the honor that comes from men. Giving glory to and seeking glory from the Father must be the center of theological study. If it's not, then theological expertise can only turn Pharisaical; it can only turn rancid. So, give glory to God and seek it from Him." We could just as surely write a similar speech entitled "The Dangers of Logic." and Leithart's words would be just as apt.

Staying stupid also means sometimes foregoing or briefly suspending logical argumentation during arguments. This sounds odd, but it is the best kind of stupid to become. While we may argue with madmen, we do not want to become one. As Chesterton says, "If you argue with a madman, it is extremely probable that you will get the worst of it; for in many ways his mind moves all the quicker for not being delayed by the things that go with good judgment. He is not hampered by a sense of humour or by charity, or by the dumb certainties of experience. He is the more logical for losing certain sane affections. Indeed, the common phrase for insanity is in this respect a misleading one. The madman is not the man who has lost his reason. The madman is the man who has lost everything except his reason." [173] Be tempered by humor and charity. Be tempered by the dumb certainties of experience. Stay stupid.

As one grows in intellectual competency and academic acumen, we must maintain a finer charm for the crowd's ear. Our goal in doing this is not to merely appeal to the popular audience because we want the approval of many. Any *ad populum* should be avoided, which is difficult in a democracy. And people-pleasing is not a Christian virtue. It is a Christian vice, centered upon one's own reputation and not on truth. Our goal in maintaining vulgar speech, the words and ideas of common man, is to appeal to the popular audience because we want the affections and friendship of many, which opens immense opportunity for further dialogue, setting a foundation for a kind reputation in future debates. Brilliant men with a heart for the people and a love for truth, over and above a heart for themselves or their academic subject, will speak the truth, but they will speak it in love, in such a way so their listeners can hear it.

What We Are To Become

Though our world is irresistibly consistent, it is not mechanical. It is poetic. In this way, it is sensical and coherent. Cause and effect is reliable, but the mystery of the world as a story in real-time can take many turns; many unexpected turns. It is riddled with paradoxes. Still, the story is reliable because its Author is moreso. Faithfully employing street-fighting logic should make us faithful characters on God's stage. It should lead to the joyful task of making many more faithful characters. It should lead us to wisdom. As Moreland says, "The spiritually mature person is a wise person. And a wise person has the savvy and skill necessary to lead an exemplary life and to address the issues of the day in a responsible, attractive way that brings honor to God...wisdom is the fruit of a life of study and a developed mind." [174]

The result of successful street-fighting Logic is not merely an ascent to true propositions or the denial of false propositions. The result is the creation of a certain kind of person, one who lives according to the truth, becoming all things to all men. Therefore, if street-fighting logic is anything, it is an incarnational logic: deeply reasonable, neither exuding the coldness of rationalism nor the emptiness of irrationalism. Logic involves more than words. It involves more than propositional ascent. It involves the passions and the credibility of an authority. It involves hope, fear, trust, sin, and the smell of roasted peanuts. It involves undying allegiances, deep preconceptions, lasting misconceptions, and basic presuppositions. Logic does not just involve the head. It involves the whole man. This is part of realizing that our thought-life, our reasoning faculties, takes place within an embodied creature. Jesus was not a proposition. Jesus was the Word made flesh. He is the *Logos*. Sometimes words are not enough. It is not that they fail. Their extension ends. This is why we have music, color, hugs, handshakes, miracles, and the laugh of a one year old. Still, in a magical way, even all these things just named are but the breath of God, the outpouring of His breath. We call it reality. When our words fail, we must rely on God's.

Let not this talk of reason's inability thwart all that has been said hitherto. Calvin brings us back into rightful balance by saying, "When we so condemn human understanding for its perpetual blindness as to leave it no perception of any object whatever, we not only go against God's Word, but also run counter to the experience of common sense. For we see implanted in human nature some sort of desire to search out the truth to which man would not at all aspire if it had not already savored it. Human understanding then possesses some power of perception, since it is by nature captivated by love of truth." [175] *Is there any poetry in Calvin?*

This then should encourage us to know that though in our employment of logic we will encounter fallen men, the image of God is such in man that even the fall did not destroy man's deep desire to know and long after truth. Reason, like all of life, may still be redeemed and will be wittingly used in the salvation, redemption, and sanctification of every saint. In short, faithfully employing street-fighting logic, the training and strategy thereof, should mature each of us further as happy Christians, and it should make others question the joy set before them. What rings true of every artist rings true of the street-fighting logician: "Even for the great artist, the most crucial work of art is his life." [176]

Focus Questions.

1. What two questions must one answer before participating in any debate?

2. What is poetic knowledge and why is it important for a proper understanding of reasoning?

3. Name a few proper motivations for participating in a debate. Name a few faulty motivations.

4. What is the difference between the imprisoned intellect and the impoverished intellect?

5. Is it enough to change someone's mind on a topic?

6. What daily disciplines promote a faithful care for the intellect?

7. Why might stupidity be considered virtuous?

8. Why is love so important for the street-fighting logician?

9. What is wrong with pressing too hard for immediate victory in a debate?

Exercises.

1. Write a 300-350 word dialogue where one participant is trying too hard to win the argument.

2. Choose your favorite quote form this chapter. Add an additional paragraph at the beginning and an additional paragraph at the end, setting up the quote and closing it out. Your words should be in the same style and tone as the original quote.

3. List five people in your life you would not think could teach you much. Write five things each of them could teach you.

Appendix

Parmenides (6th century B.C.)

"One should both say and think that Being Is; for To Be is possible, and Nothingness is not possible…For this (view) can never predominate, that That Which Is Not exists. You must debar your thought from this way of search, nor let ordinary experience in its variety force you along this way (namely, that of allowing) the eye, sightless as it is, and the ear, full of sound, and the tongue, to rule; but (you must) judge by means of the Reason (Logos) the much contested proof which is expounded by me." [177]

Euripides (480–406 B.C.)

"You won't hear me asking which gods exist
or cross-examining their actions.
I hold with those hardy traditions
we inherit from our fathers –
their roots go deep, they're old as time.
The wisest man living, though he brings
to bear his keenest logic,
will never break their grip on our lives." [178]

Plato (427-347 B.C.)

"[Socrates speaking during the dialogue with Theaetetus about the nature of knowledge and truth] For if truth is only sensation, and no man can discern another's feelings better than he, or has any superior right to determine whether his opinion is true or false, but each, as we have several times repeated, is to himself the sole judge, and everything that he judges is true and right, why, my friend should Protagoras be preferred to the place of wisdom and instruction, and deserve to be well paid, and we poor ignoramuses have to go to him, if each one is the measure of his own wisdom?" [179]

"Now, it looks as though the other so-called virtues of the soul are akin to those of the body, for they really aren't there beforehand but are added later by habit and practice. However, the virtue of reason seems to belong above all to something more divine, which never loses its power but is either useful and beneficial or useless and harmful, depending on the way it is turned. Or have you never noticed this about people who are said to be vicious but clever, how keen the vision of their little souls is and how sharply it distinguishes the things it is turned towards? This shows that its sight isn't inferior but rather is forced to serve evil ends, so that the sharper it sees, the more evil it accomplishes." [180]

Aristotle (384-322 B.C.)

"You should display your training in inductive reasoning against a young man, in deductive against an expert. You should try, moreover, to secure from those skilled in deduction their premises, from inductive reasoners their parallel cases; for this is the thing in which they are respectively trained. In general, too, from your exercises in argumentation you should try to carry away either a syllogism on some subject or a refutation or a proposition or an objection, or whether some one put his question properly or improperly (whether it was yourself or someone else) and the point which made it the one or the other." [181]

St. Augustine of Hippo (354 AD – 430):

A Prayer Before Study adopted from St. Augustine
O Thou who art the Light of the minds that know Thee
the Life of the souls that love Thee
the Strength of the wills that serve Thee
Help us to know Thee that we may truly love thee,
So to love thee that we may fully serve Thee
Whose service is perfect freedom.

"The science of reasoning is of very great service in searching into and unraveling all sorts of questions that come up in Scripture, only in the use of it we must guard against the love of wrangling and the childish vanity of entrapping an adversary. For there are many of what are called *sophisms*, inferences in reasoning that are false, and yet so close an imitation of the true, as to deceive not only dull people, but clever men too, when they are not on their guard." [182]

St. Thomas Aquinas (1225 – 1274):

"We have a more perfect knowledge of God by grace than by natural reason. Which appears thus. The knowledge which we have by natural reason requires two things: phantasms received from the sensible objects, and the natural intelligible light, by whose power we abstract from them intelligible concepts. Now in both of these human knowledge is assisted by the revelation of grace. For the intellect's natural light is strengthened by the infusion of gratuitous light. And sometimes also the phantasms in the human imagination are divinely formed, so as to express divine things better than those do which we receive from sensible things, as appears in prophetic visions; while sometimes sensible things, or even voices, are divinely formed to express some thing divine, as in the Baptism, the Holy Ghost was seen in the shape of a dove, and the voice of the Father was heard, *This is My beloved Son* (Matt. 3:17)." [183]

"Hilary says (*De Trin.* i), 'Let not man think to reach the sacrament of generation by his own mind.' And Ambrose says (*De Fide* i, 10), 'It is impossible to know the secret of generation. The mind fails, the voice is silent.' But the trinity of the divine persons is distinguished by origin of regeneration and procession (Q. XXX, A. 2). Since, therefore, man cannot know, and with his understanding graps that for which no necessary reason can be given, it follows that the trinity of persons cannot be known by reason." [184]

A Prayer Before Study adopted from Thomas Aquinas:
O God, Creator of all that is, from the treasures of Your wisdom,

You have arrayed the universe with marvelous order, and now govern with skill and might.

You are the true found of light and wisdom.

Pour forth a ray of your brightness into the darkened places of our minds; disperse our souls of the two fold darkness into which we were born: sin and ignorance. Grant to each us of us deftness of hand, keeness of mind, skill in learning, subtlety to interpret, and eloquence in speech.

May you guide the beginning of our work, direct its progress, and bring it to completion.

You who bring all that is good to its proper end, Now prosper the work of our hands,

Through Jesus Christ our Lord, Amen.[185]

John Calvin (1509 - 1564):

"…in order that the great nobility of our race (which distinguishes us from brute beasts) may not be buried beneath our own dullness of wit, it behooves us to recognize that we have been endowed with reason and understanding so that, by leading a holy and upright life, we may press on to the appointed goal of blessed immortality." [186]

"For, while men dispute among themselves about the individual sections of the law, they agree on the general conception of equity. In this respect the frailty of the human mind is surely proved: even when it seems to follow the way, it limps and staggers. Yet the fact remains that some seed of political order has been implanted in all men. And this is ample proof that in the arrangement of this life no man is without the light of reason." [187]

"…let it be enough for us that the understanding is, as it were, the leader and governor of the soul; and that the will is always mindful of the bidding of the understanding, and in its own desires awaits the judgment of the understanding…Therefore God provided man's soul with a mind, by which to distinguish good from evil, right from wrong; and, with the light of reason as guide, to distinguish what should be followed from what should be avoided." [188]

John Owen (1616 – 1683):

"From the description we have in Romans 7, lust darkens the mind, extinguishes conflictions, dethrones reason, interrupts the power and influences that resist it, and then breaks out into an open flame." [189]

Isaac Watts (1674 - 1748):

"God is the God of light and truth, a God of reason and order, and he never requires mankind to use their natural faculties amiss for the support of his cause. Even the most mysterious and sublime doctrines of revelation are not to be believed with a just reason for it; nor should our pious affections be engaged in the defence of them, till we have plain and convincing proof that they are certainly revealed, though perhaps we may never in this world attain to such clear and distinct ideas of them as we desire." [190]

John Henry Cardinal Newman (1801 - 1890):

"Logic is the organization of thought, and, as being such, is a security for the faithfulness of intellectual developments; and the necessity of using it is undeniable as far as this, that its rules must not be transgressed. That it is not brought into exercise in every instance of doctrinal development is owing to the varieties of mental constitution, whether in communities or in individuals, with whom great truths or seeming truths are lodged. The question indeed may be asked whether a development can be other in any case than a logical operation; but, if by this is meant a conscious reasoning from premises to conclusion, of course the answer must be in the negative." [191]

Soren Kierkegaard (1813 - 1855):

"It is the business of reason to eliminate everything that is only an apparent paradox and to free us once and for all from that which is *not* Absurd. Then, when the Absurd stands forth in all its naked clarity, then what? Why then the reason will in no wise be able to show that the Absurd is nonsense. But neither will it be able to master the Absurd, to prove its logical necessity speculatively or its incontestable actuality historically." *Papirer*

Frances R. Havergal (1836 - 1879):

Take my silver and my gold,
Not a mite would I withhold.

Take my intellect and use
Every pow'r as Thou shalt choose.

Herman Bavinck (1854 - 1921):

"Scripture urges us to behold heaven and earth, birds and ants, flowers and lilies, in order that we may see and recognize God in them…Scripture does not reason in the abstract. It does not make God the conclusion of a syllogism, leaving it to us whether we think the argument holds or not. But it speaks with authority. Both theologically and religiously it proceeds from God as the starting point. We receive the impression that belief in the existence of God is based entirely upon these proofs. But indeed that would be 'a wretched faith, which, before it invokes God, must first prove his existence.' The contrary, however, is the truth. There is not a single object of existence of which we hesitate to accept until definite proofs are furnished. Of the existence of self, of the world round about us, of logical and moral laws, etc., we are so deeply convinced because of the indelible impressions with all these things make upon our consciousness that we need no arguments or demonstrations. Spontaneously, altogether involuntarily: without any constraint or coercion, we accept that existence. Now the same is true in regard to the existence of God. The so-called proofs are by no means the final grounds of our most certain conviction that God exists. This certainty is established only by faith; that is, by the spontaneous testimony which forces itself upon us from every side." [192]

G.K. Chesterton (1874 - 1936)

"The whole secret of mysticism is this: that man can understand everything by the help of what he does not understand. The morbid logician seeks to make everything lucid, and succeeds in making everything mysterious. The mystic allows one thing to be mysterious, and everything else becomes lucid. [193]

"The creeds and the crusades, the hierarchies and the horrible persecutions were not organized, as is ignorantly said, for the suppression of reason. They were organized for the difficult defense of reason." [194]

J. Gresham Machen (1881 – 1937):

"God usually exerts that power in connection with certain prior conditions of the human mind, and it should be ours to create, so far as we can, with the help of God, those favourable conditions for the reception of the gospel. False ideas are the greatest obstacles to the reception of the gospel. We may preach with all the fervor of a reformer and yet succeed only in winning a straggler here or there, if we permit the whole collective thought of the nation or of the world to be controlled by ideas which, by the resistless force of logic, prevent Christianity from being regarded as anything more than a harmless delusion." [195]

Henri de Lubac (1896 - 1991):

"Man…is 'in the image of God,' not merely because of his intellect, his free will, his immortality, not even because of the power he has to rule over nature: beyond and above all this, he is so ultimately because there is something incomprehensible in his depths." [196]

Herbert Schlossberg:

"In their uncompromising determination to proclaim truth, Christians must avoid the intellectual flabbiness of the larger society. They must rally against the prevailing distrust of reason and the exaltation of the irrational. Emotional self-indulgence and irrationalities have always been the enemies of the gospel, and the apostles warned their followers against them." [197]

Alvin Plantinga (1932 – Present):

"[Argument-based faith] could be bothersome and time consuming; and what do I do if someone does find a flaw in my argument? Stop going to church? From Calvin's point of view believing in the existence of God on the basis of rational argument is like believing in the existence of your spouse on the basis of the analogical argument for other minds – whimsical at best and unlikely to delight the person concerned." [198]

"...what about the belief that there is such a person as God and that we are responsible to him? Is that among the deliverances of reason or an item of faith? For Calvin it is clearly the former. 'There is within the human mind, and indeed by natural instinct, an awareness of divinity. ... God himself has implanted in all men a certain understanding of his divine majesty. ... men one and all perceive that there is a God and that he is their Maker." (Institutes I, 3, 1) According to Calvin everyone, whether in the faith or not, has a tendency or nisus, in certain situations, to apprehend God's existence and to grasp something of his nature and actions. This natural knowledge can be and is suppressed by sin, but the fact remains that a capacity to apprehend God's existence is as much part of our natural noetic equipment as is the capacity to apprehend perceptual truths, truths about the past, and truths about other minds. Belief in the existence of God is in the same boat as belief in other minds, the past and perceptual objects; in each case God has so constructed us that in the right circumstances we form the belief in question. But then the belief that there is such a person as God is as much among the deliverances of reason as those other beliefs. From this vantage point we can see, therefore, that the Reformed epistemologist is not a fideist at all with respect to belief in God. He does not hold that there is any conflict between faith and reason here, and he does not even hold that we cannot attain this fundamental truth by reason, he holds, instead, that it is among the deliverances of reason." [199]

Notes

[1] Isaac Watts, in his Letter to Sir John Hartopp published in *Logic or the Right Use of Reason in the Inquiry after Truth*. London; August 24, 1724.

[2] Chesterton, G K. *The Collected Works of G.k. Chesterton*. Charlottesville, Va: InteLex Corp, 2002. Print. Volume 1, 196.

[3] Kreeft, Peter. *Socratic Logic, Edition 3.1*. South Bend: St. Augustine's Press, 2010. Print, 23

[4] Moreland, James P, and Dallas Willard. *Love Your God with All Your Mind: The Role of Reason in the Life of the Soul*. Colorado Springs, Colo: NavPress, 1997. Print, 21.

[5] Inscription on the bench of the Albert Einstein Memorial in Washington, D.C.

[6] Kreeft, *Socratic Logic*, ix.

[7] Sayers, Dorothy L. *The Lost Tools of Learning*. New York: National Review, 1961. Print, 14.

[8] Hopkins, Jasper, Nicholas, and Johannes Wenck. *Nicholas of Cusa's Debate with John Wenck: A Translation and an Appraisal of De Ignota Litteratura and Apologia Doctae Ignorantiae*. Minneapolis: A.J. Banning Press, 1988. Print, 474.

[9] Roberts, Alexander, and James Donaldson. *The Ante-Nicene Fathers: Translations of the Writings of the Fathers Down to A.d. 325*. Grand Rapids: W.B. Eerdmans Pub. Co, 1950. Print, 163.

[10] Moreland, *Love Your God with All Your Mind, 32.*

[11] Ibid., 15.

[12] Ibid., 33.

[13] Watts, *Logic or the Right Use of Reason in the Inquiry after Truth,* 5.

[14] Frame, John M. *The Doctrine of the Christian Life.* Phillipsburg, N.J.: P & R Pub, 2008. Print, 366.

[15] Hutchins, Robert M. *Great Books of the Western World, Volume 18.* Encyclopaedia Britannica, Inc, 1900. Print, 652.

[16] Nance, James B, and Douglas Wilson. *Introductory Logic for Christian and Home Schools.* Moscow, Idaho: Canon Press, 2006. Print.

[17] Poythress, Vern S. *Logic: A God-Centered Approach to the Foundation of Western Thought.* Wheaton, Ill: Crossway, 2013. Print, 27-32.

[18] Hutchins, Robert M. *Great Books of the Western World, Volume 19.* Encyclopaedia Britannica, Inc, 1900. Print, 3.

[19] Calvin, John and Robert M. Hutchins. *Great Books of the Western World, Vol. 20.* Chicago: Encyclopaedia Britannica, 1952. Print, 193.

[20] Wesley, John. "An Address to Clergy," in The Works of John Wesley, 3d ed. Grand Rapids: Baker, 1979; is ted., 1972, 481.

[21] Orr, James, *The Christian View of God and the World* (Grand Rapids: Eerdmans, 1954; 1st ed., 1893, 20-21.

[22] Chesterton, G K. *Orthodoxy.* San Francisco: Ignatius, 1995. Print, 22.

[23] Lewis, C.S. *Mere Christianity.* New York: Macmillan, 1943; rev. ed., 1952, 75.

[24] Kreeft, *Socratic Logic,* 1.

[25] Watts, *Logic or the Right Use of Reason in the Inquiry after Truth,* 1.

[26] Runes, Dagobert D. *Classics in Logic: Readings in Epistemology, Theory of Knowledge and Dialectics*. New York: Philosophical Library, 1962. Print, 65.

[27] Cicerón, Marco T, Marco T. Cicerón, Niall Rudd, and Jonathan Powell. *The Republic, and the Laws*. Oxford: Oxford University Press, 2008. Print, 27.

[28] Runes, 310.

[29] Petrarca, Francesco, James H. Robinson, and Henry W. Rolfe. *Petrarch, the First Modern Scholar and Man of Letters: A Selection from His Correspondence with Boccaccio and Other Friends, Designed to Illustrate the Beginnings of the Renaissance*. New York: G.P. Putnam's Sons, 1898. Print.

[30] Runes, 360.

[31] Kreeft, *Socratic Logic*, 1.

[32] Watts, *Logic or the Right Use of Reason in the Inquiry after Truth*, iii.

[33] Ibid., 5.

[34] Ibid. 6.

[35] Augustine, , and Henry Chadwick. *Confessions*. Oxford: Oxford University Press, 2008. Print, 10.23.33.

[36] See also Psalm 111:10 and Prov. 9:10.

[37] Agustín, , and R.P.H Green. *On Christian Teaching*. Oxford: Oxford University Press, 2011. Print, 34.

[38] Frame, 367.

[39] Ibid.

[40] Chesterton, *Orthodoxy*, 38.

[41] Roberts and Donaldson, 177.

[42] Hutchins, *Great Books of the Western World*. Volume 19. Q12, Article 12, *Summa Theologica*, 61.

[43] Augustine, *On Christian Teaching*, 46.

[44] Boersma, Hans. *Heavenly Participation: The Weaving of a Sacramental Tapestry*. Grand Rapids, Mich: W.B. Eerdmans Pub. Co, 2011. Print, 24.

[45] Ibid., 21.

[46] Hutchins, *Great Books of the Western World*. Volume 19. Q102, Article 1, *Summa Theologica*, 523.

[47] Frame, 367.

[48] Ibid.

[49] Klassen, Norman, and Jens Zimmermann. *The Passionate Intellect: Incarnational Humanism and the Future of University Education*. Grand Rapids, Mich: Baker Academic, 2006. Print, 157-158.

[50] McDurmon, Joel. *Biblical Logic in Theory & Practice: Refuting the Fallacies of Humanism, Darwinism, Atheism, and Just Plain Stupidity*. Powder Springs, Ga: American Vision, 2009. Print, 10.

[51] Watts, *Logic or the Right Use of Reason in the Inquiry after Truth*, 6.

[52] Schaeffer, Francis A, and Francis A. Schaeffer. *Art and the Bible*. Downers Grove, Ill: IVP Books, 2006. Print, 38.

[53] Watts, Isaac. *The Improvement of the Mind; Or, a Supplement to the Art of Logic: Containing a Variety of Remarks and Rules for the Attainment and Communication of Useful Knowledge in Religion, the Sciences, and in Common Life*. Washington, DC: American Psychological Association, 2010. Print, 7.

[54] Lewis, C S. *The Complete C.s. Lewis Signature Classics*. New York, NY: HarperOne, 2007. Print, 185.

[55] Lewis, C S. *Reflections on the Psalms*. New York: Harcourt, Brace, 1958. Print, 7.

[56] Watts, *The Improvement of the Mind*, 15.

[57] Ibid., 16-17.

[58] Ibid., 29-30.

[59] Ibid., 30.

[60] Ibid., 31.

[61] Ibid., 30-31.

[62] Moreland, 53-54.

[63] Watts, *The Improvement of the Mind*, 9.

[64] Petrarch, Francis. James Harvey Robinson transl. *From a Letter to Boccaccio.* New York and London: G.P. Putnam's Sons. 1898.

[65] Petrarch, Francis. Jaboc Zeitlin transl. *The Life of Solitude.* Chicago: University of Illinois Press, 1924.

[66] Ibid.

[67] Moreland, 54.

[68] Watts, *The Improvement of the Mind,* 43.

[69] Foster, Richard J. *Celebration of Discipline.* Hodder & Stoughton, 1989. Print, 55.

[70] Watts, *The Improvement of the Mind,* 48.

[71] Ibid., 43-44.

[72] Ibid., 6.

[73] Ibid., 48.

[74] Ibid., 41.

[75] Cassirer, Ernst, Paul O. Kristeller, and John H. Randall. *Petrarca, Valla, Ficino, Pico, Pomponazzi, Vives: The Renaissance Philosophy of Man : (3. Print.).* Chicago, Ill, 1954. Print, 47.

[76] Watts, *The Improvement of the Mind,* 4.

[77] Calvin, 242.

[78] Watts, *The Improvement of the Mind,* 1.

[79] Watts, *The Improvement of the Mind,* 5.

[80] Cassirer, 34.

[81] Watts, *The Improvement of the Mind,* 82.

[82] Ibid., 103-104.

[83] Schaeffer, *Art and the Bible,* 17.

[84] Augustine, *Confessions,* 88.

[85] Edwards, Jonathan, J M. Houston, and Jonathan Edwards. *Faith Beyond Feelings: Discerning the Heart of True Spirituality.* Colorado Springs, Colo: Victor, 2005. Print, 17.

[86] Lewis, *Reflections on the Psalms,* 14.

[87] Scheler, Max. *Formalism in Ethics and Non-Formal Ethics of Values: A New Attempt Toward the Foundation of an Ethical*

Personalism. Evanston: Northwestern University Press, 1973. Print, 285.

[88] Kreeft, *Socratic Logic*, 108.

[89] Adler, Mortimer J. *How to Speak, How to Listen.* , 1983. Print, 5.

[90] Watts, *The Improvement of the Mind*, 80

[91] Adler, *How to Speak How to Listen*, 92.

[92] Augustine, *On Christian Teaching*, 31.

[93] McDurmon, 11.

[94] Watts, *The Improvement of the Mind*, 95.

[95] Ibid., 85.

[96] Ibid., 91.

[97] Ibid.

[98] Ibid., 92.

[99] Sidney, Philip, and Gavin Alexander. *Sidney's 'the Defence of Poesy' and Selected Renaissance Literary Criticism*. London: Penguin, 2004. Print, 15-16.

[100] Watts, *The Improvement of the Mind*, 93.

[101] Ibid.

[102] Chesterton, *Orthodoxy*, 14.

[103] Lewis, *Reflections on the Psalms*, 73.

[104] Calvin, 280-281.

[105] Augustine, *Confessions*, 78.

[106] Moreland, 133-134.

[107] Watts, *The Improvement of the Mind*, 84.

[108] Ibid., 116.

[109] Ibid., 95.

[110] Ibid., 97.

[111] Augustine, *Confessions*, 77-78.

[112] Ibid., 78.

[113] Watts, *The Improvement of the Mind*, 87.

[114] Ibid., 87-88

[115] Calvin, 185.

[116] Watts, *The Improvement of the Mind*, 83.

[117] Ibid., 84.

[118] Augustine, *Confessions*, 68..

[119] Plantinga, Alvin, and Nicholas Wolterstorff. *Faith and Rationality: Reason and Belief in God*. Notre Dame: University of Notre Dame Press, 1983. Print, 155.

[120] Runes, 66.

[121] Watts, *The Improvement of the Mind*, 101.

[122] Ibid., 76.

[123] Chesterton, *Orthodoxy*, 14.

[124] Watts, *The Improvement of the Mind*, 81.

[125] Watts, *The Improvement of the Mind*, 86.

[126] Lewis, *Reflections on the Psalms*, 73.

[127] Hopkins, Jasper. "Prolegomena to Nicholas of Cusa's Conception of the Relationship of Faith to Reason." 1996. Web. 13 Sept. 2013. <http://jasper-hopkins.info/cusafaith_reason-engl.pdf>.

[128] Lewis, *Reflections on the Psalms*, 28.

[129] Ibid., 46.

[130] Cowan, Louise, and Os Guinness. *Invitation to the Classics*. Grand Rapids, Mich: Baker Books, 1998. Print, 20.

[131] Wilson, Douglas, Wesley Callihan, and Douglas Jones. *Classical Education & the Home School*. Moscow, Idaho: Canon Press, 2001. Print, 27-28.

[132] Augustine, *Confessions*, 96.

[133] Chesterton, *Orthodoxy*, 13.

[134] Sidney, 17-18.

[135] Lewis, *Reflections on the Psalms*, 73.

[136] Augustine, *Confessions*, 3.

[137] O'Connor, Flannery, and Sally Fitzgerald. *The Habit of Being: Letters*. New York: Farrar, Straus, Giroux, 1979. Print, 134.

[138] Augustine, *Confessions*, 7.10.16.

[139] Hopkins, Jasper. "Prolegomena to Nicholas of Cusa's Conception of the Relationship of Faith to Reason." 12.

[140] Schaeffer, Francis A. *Escape from Reason*. London: Inter-Varsity Fellowship, 1968. Print, 108.

[141] Kreeft, *Socratic Logic*, 2.

[142] McDurmon, 10.

[143] Kreeft, *Socratic Logic*, 108-109.

[144] Maritain, Jacques. *The Range of Reason*. New York: Scribner, 1952. Print, 18-25.

[145] Taylor, James S. *Poetic Knowledge: The Recovery of Education*. Albany, N.Y: State University of New York Press, 1998. Print, 5-6.

[146] Pieper, Josef, and Josef Pieper. *Leisure: The Basis of Culture ; the Philosophical Act*. San Francisco: Ignatius Press, 2009. Print, 18.

[147] Wilson, Douglas, and Nathan D. Wilson. *The Rhetoric Companion: A Student's Guide to Power in Persuasion*. Moscow, Idaho: Canon Press, 2011. Print, 83-84.

[148] Calvin, 284.

[149] Moreland, 24.

[150] Chesterton, G K. *The Collected Works of G.k. Chesterton*. Charlottesville, Va: InteLex Corp, 2002. Print. Volume III, 171.

[151] Stott, John R. W. *Your Mind Matters: The Place of the Mind in the Christian Life*. Downers Grove: InterVarsity Press, 2006. Print, 18.

[152] Edwards, 17.

[153] Ibid.

[154] McNeill, John T, and Ford L. Battles. *Calvin: Institutes of the Christian Religion*. Philadelphia, PA: Westminster Press, 1960. Print, 79.

[155] Calvin, 270-271.

[156] Stott, 25.

[157] Chesterton, *Orthodoxy*, 26-27.

[158] Edwards, 131-141.

[159] Ibid., 139.

[160] Calvin, 40.

[161] Poythress, 44.   *see p. 178, on footnote #17*

[162] Moreland, 24.

[163] Hall, Douglas C. *The Trinity: An Anlysis of St. Thomas Aquinas' "expositio" of the "de Trintate" of Boethius.* Leiden [etc.: E. J. Brill, 1992. Print, 68.

[164] Ibid., 72.

[165] Nash, Ronald H. *The Word of God and the Mind of Man.* Phillipsburg, N.J: P & R Pub, 1992. Print, 93.

[166] Ibid., 99.

[167] Ibid., 109.

[168] Schaeffer, *Escape from Reason,* 117.

[169] Benson, Thomas W, and Michael H. Prosser. *Readings in Classical Rhetoric.* Davis, Calif: Hermagoras, 1988. Print, 150.

[170] Ibid.

[171] Ibid., 49.

[172] Ibid., 162.

[173] Chesterton, *Orthodoxy,* 22.

[174] Moreland, 39.

[175] Calvin, 271.

[176] Schaeffer, *Art and the Bible,* 49.

[177] Runes, 590.

[178] Corrigan, Robert W. *Classical Tragedy, Greek and Roman: 8 Plays in Authoritative Modern Translations Accompanied by Critical Essays.* New York, N.Y: Applause Theatre Book Publishers, 1990. Print, 378.

[179] Runes, 628.

[180] Plato, , G M. A. Grube, and C D. C. Reeve. *Republic.* Indianapolis: Hackett Pub. Co, 1992. Print, 190-191.

[181] Pickard-Cambridge, W A. *Topics.* Place of publication not identified: Digireads Com, 2006. Print, book VIII, chapter 14.

[182] Hutchins, *Great Books of the Western World.* Volume 18, 651.

[183] Hutchins, *Great Books of the Western World.* Volume 19. Q12, Article 13, *Summa Theologica.*

[184] Ibid., Q32, A 1 175d-178a.

[185] Thomas is one of the heaviest hitters in Christian church history on the role of reason and the intellect in the Christian life. Aquinas begins his *Summa Theologica* with a defense of why Theology as a separate science is not only needed, but imperative. He weaves throughout his articles and objections many great discussions on the range and role of reason. The whole *Summa* stands on this distinction.

[186] Calvin, 242.

[187] Ibid., 273.

[188] Ibid., 194-195.

[189] Owen, John. *The Mortification of Sin*. Edinburgh: Banner of Truth Trust, 2004. Print, 33.

[190] Watts, *The Improvement of the Mind*, 179.

[191] Newman, John H. *An Essay on the Development of Christian Doctrine*. Notre Dame, Ind: University of Notre Dame Press, 1989. Print, chapter five, section 4.

[192] Bavinck, Herman. William Hendrickson transl. *The Doctrine of God*. Grand Rapids: Eerdmans, 1951, 78-79.

[193] Chesterton, *Orthodoxy*, 33.

[194] Chesterton, *Orthodoxy*, 39.

[195] Delivered September 20, 1912, 101st session of Princeton Theological Seminary. Reprinted in J. Gresham Machen, *What is Christianity?* Grand Rapids: Eerdmans, 1951.

[196] Lubac, Henri . *The Mystery of the Supernatural*. New York: Herder and Herder, 1967. Print, 209-210.

[197] Schlossberg, Herbert. *Idols for Destruction*. Nashville: Nelson, 1983, 322.

[198] Plantinga, 67.

[199] Plantinga, 89-90.